Being Nobody, Going Nowhere

Being Nobody, Going Nowhere

Ayya Khema

Wisdom Publications · London

First published in 1987

Wisdom Publications, 23 Dering Street, London W1, England

© Ayya Khema 1987

British Library Cataloguing in Publication Data
Khema, Ayya
  Being nobody, going nowhere.
  1. Spiritual life (Buddhism)
  I. Title
  294.3'444   BQ4302

ISBN 0 86171 052 5

Set in Palatino 10 on 12½ point by Character
Graphics of Taunton, Somerset, and printed and
bound by Eurasia Press of Singapore on 80 gsm cream
Sunningdale Opaque paper supplied by Link
Publishing Papers of West Byfleet, Surrey.

Contents

Preface

This is a simple book for ordinary people who want to find greater happiness and contentment in their lives by following a spiritual path. The Buddha's path is simple and meant for ordinary people, and anyone with goodwill and determination can follow its steps towards freedom of heart and mind. Both heart and mind have to be involved in this journey towards liberation from the 'self.' The mind understands and concludes, connects and discerns, whereas the heart feels.

When our feelings become free of emotional reactions and dwell in love and compassion as their natural abode, our mind will be open to the great truths of universal significance. And the more we refer to these truths, the closer we will get to spiritual emancipation. Hopefully this book can help to point out some steps on the way, according to the Buddha's teaching, and facilitate the journey.

A ten-day meditation course in Kundasale, Sri Lanka was the venue for the talks, that are published here. Although my name appears as the author, this book could never have been assembled without the help and support of many people, each making their own special contribution.

The students on the course provided the impetus for the talks and their questions occasioned many of the points mentioned. Stanley Wijegunawardena was the manager and convener of the course and without him this book would not have been possible.

Barbara Raif transcribed the tapes and Sister Sanghamittā typed the first edited version. Sister Vayāmā proof-read the manuscript. Katja and Amara looked after my physical well-being, and Helga gave me massages and moral support.

All the supporters in Sri Lanka, especially Mr Arthur de Silva, made it possible for me to have the peace and quiet in my hut to attend to this book.

How can I show my gratitude? If this book helps even one person to find their path to freedom, the effort will have been amply rewarded.

AYYA KHEMA
Parappuduwa Nuns Island
Dodanduwa, Sri Lanka
October, 1985

1 *Meditation – Why and How*

Why is meditation so important? You must have realized that it is, otherwise you wouldn't be here. I'd like to emphasize that meditation is not just something extra to be done in our spare time, but is essential for our well-being.

One of our human absurdities is the fact that we're constantly thinking about either the future or the past. Those who are young think of the future because they've got more of it. Those who are older think more about the past because for them there is more of that. But in order to experience life, we have to live each moment. Life has not been happening in the past. That's memory. Life is not going to happen in the future. That's planning. The only time we can live is now, this moment, and as absurd as it may seem, we've got to learn that. As human beings with life spans of sixty, seventy or eighty years we have to learn to actually experience living in the present. When we have learned that, we will have eliminated a great many of our problems.

How simple it sounds, how difficult it is. Anyone who has been trying knows that. Those of you who haven't tried yet will certainly find out. Such a simple premise and not at all easy to do. There's no other way to learn to live each moment except through meditation. Meditation has other aspects and facets which also help us to do that.

We are all quite able and efficient in looking after our bodies. We wash them at least once a day, probably even more often. We go out with clean clothes. We rest our bodies at night. Everyone has a bed. We wouldn't be able to stand up to the strain of living if we didn't also rest. We have a house where we shelter the body from rain, wind, sun, the heat and the cold. We wouldn't be able to function well otherwise. We feed the body with healthy nourishment, not with anything that we would consider poison. We give it the food we consider good for us and we take exercise. At least we walk. If we didn't, our legs would atrophy and we could no longer use them. Exactly the same has to be done for the mind.

In fact it's even more important because the mind is the master and the body is the servant. The best servant in perfect condition, young, strong and vigorous, having a weak and dissolute master who doesn't know what to do, will not be able to work satisfactorily. The master has to direct the servant. Even when the servant isn't so strong and vigorous, if the master is efficient and wise the household will still be in order.

This mind and body is our household. If this inner household is not in order, no outer household can be in order. The one we live and work in is dependent on the order that we have created in our own inner household. The master, the one in charge, has to be in the best possible condition.

Nothing in the whole universe is comparable to the mind or can take its place. Everything is mind-made. Yet we all take our minds for granted, which is another absurdity. No one takes the body for granted. When the body gets sick, we quickly run to the doctor. When the body gets hungry, we quickly feed it. When the body gets tired, we quickly rest it. But what about the mind? Only the meditator looks after the mind.

Looking after the mind is essential if life is to grow in depth and vision. Otherwise life stays two-dimensional. Most lives are lived in the realities of yesterday and tomorrow, good and bad, I like it and I don't like it, I'll have it and I won't have it, this is mine and this is yours. Only when the mind is trained can we see other dimensions.

The first thing we need to do with the mind is wash it, clean it up, not only once or twice a day as we do for the body but in all our waking moments. In order to do that, we have to learn how. With the body it's very simple, we use soap and water. We learned to do that when we were small. Mind can only be cleansed by mind. What the mind has put in there, the mind can take out. One second of concentration in meditation is one second of purification because, luckily, the mind can only do one thing at a time. Although, as the Buddha said, we can have three thousand mind moments in the blink of an eyelid, we don't usually have that many and we don't have them all at once. Mind moments follow each other in quick succession but only one at a time.

When we concentrate, the five hindrances, our defilements, don't get a chance to arise because the mind can only do one thing at a time. And as we get better at enlarging our periods of concentration the mind gets cleansed of its rough spots.

Our mind, that unique tool in all the universe, is the only one we have. If we owned a fine tool we would obviously look after it. We'd polish it and remove any rust. We'd sharpen it, we'd oil it and we'd rest it from time to time. Here we have this marvellous tool with which everything can be accomplished, including enlightenment, and it's up to us to learn to look after it. It won't function properly otherwise.

During meditation we learn to drop from the mind what we don't want to keep. We only want to keep in mind our meditation subject. As we become more and more skilled at it, we start to use the same faculty in our daily lives to help us drop those thoughts which are unwholesome. In this way our meditation practice assists us in daily living and our attention to wholesome thoughts in everyday life helps our meditation practice. The person who becomes master of his or her own thoughts and learns to think what they want to think is called an Arahant, an Enlightened One.

Please don't be surprised if this letting go of thoughts doesn't work all the time; it will surely function some of the time. It is an immense release and relief when one can think, even for one moment, what one wants to think, because then one has become master of the mind instead of the mind being the master of oneself. Being involved in whatever thoughts arise, unhappy or happy ones, in constant flux and flow – this is what we learn to drop when we manage to stay on the meditation subject.

Our second step is exercising the mind. An untrained mind is like a wavering, fluctuating mass which runs from one subject to the next and finds it very difficult to stay in one spot. You have probably had the experience when reading a book of coming to the end of a page and, realizing you don't know what you've just read, having to read the whole page over again. The mind has to be pushed to stay in one spot, like doing press-ups, like weight lifting, developing muscles in the mind. Strength can only come from exercising the mind to do exactly what one wants it to do, to stand still when one wants it to stand still.

This also creates power in the mind because it's connected with renunciation, with letting go. All of us, not being Arahants, have sizeable egos. The 'me' and 'mine' syndrome and 'if you please, I'll keep it and you stay out' attitudes create all the world's problems. We can only be sure that the ego is affirmed when we're thinking, talking, reading, seeing a movie or using the mind in the interests of ego. The great renunciation that arises in meditation is to drop all thoughts. When there's nobody thinking there's no ego confirmation.

To start with, dropping thoughts will only be possible momentarily but it is a step in the right direction. The spiritual path is all about letting go. There is nothing to achieve or gain. Although these words are used frequently, they are only ways of expressing ourselves. In reality a spiritual path is a path of renunciation, letting go, constantly dropping all we have built up around ourselves. This includes possessions, conditioned habits, ideas, beliefs, thinking patterns. It is difficult to stop thinking in meditation because that would be like renunciation and it is a moment when the ego doesn't have any support. When it happens for the first time, the mind immediately reacts with: 'Oh, what was that?' and – of course – one is thinking again.

To be able to keep the mind in one spot creates mind muscles, gives the mind strength and power. The teaching of the Buddha is profound and extraordinary, and only a profound and extraordinary mind can actually understand the inner vision of what he meant. Therefore we need to train the mind towards that goal.

The body's strength makes it possible to acccomplish what we set out to do with the body. The mind's strength makes it possible to do the same with the mind. A strong mind does not suffer from boredom, frustration, depression or unhappiness – it has learned to drop what it doesn't want. Meditation practice has given it the necessary muscles.

The mind, being the most valuable and intricate tool in the universe, also needs a rest. We have been thinking ever since we were very small and innumerable lifetimes before that.

All day we think, all night we dream. There isn't a moment's rest. We may go on holiday but what goes on holiday? The body goes on holiday. It might go to the beach, to the seaside or the mountains or to a different country, but what about the mind? Instead of thinking about the work one has to do at home, one thinks about all the sights, sounds and tastes at the new place. The mind isn't getting a holiday. It just thinks about something else.

If we didn't give the body a rest at night, it wouldn't function very long. Our mind needs a rest too, but this can't be had through sleeping. The only time the mind can have a real rest is when it stops thinking and starts only experiencing. One of the similes used for the mind is a blank screen on which a continuous film is shown without intermission. Because the film – the thoughts – is continuous, one forgets that there has to be a screen behind on which to project it.

If we stop that film for a moment in meditation we can experience the basic purity of our mind. That is a moment of bliss. A moment which brings the kind of happiness not available anywhere else, through anything else. A happiness which is independent of outer conditions. It's not unconditioned but conditioned only by concentration. It's not dependent upon good food or climate, entertainment or the right relationships, other people or pleasant responses or possessions, all of which are totally unreliable and cannot be depended upon because they are always changing. Concentration is reliable if one keeps practising.

Once verbalization stops for a moment, not only is there quiet but there is a feeling of contentment. The mind has at last found its home. We wouldn't be very happy if we didn't have a home for this body of ours. We are equally not very happy if we haven't got a home for the mind. That quiet, peaceful space is the mind's home. It can go home and relax just as we do after a day's work when we relax the body in an easy chair and at night in a bed. Now the mind, too, can take it easy. It doesn't have to think. Thinking is suffering, no matter what it is that we think. There is movement in it and because of that there is friction. Everything that moves creates friction.

The moment we relax and rest the mind it gains new

strength and also happiness because it knows it can go home at any time. The happiness created at the time of meditation carries through to daily living because the mind knows that nothing has to be taken so seriously that it can't go home again and find peace and quiet.

These are the main reasons why life can never be fulfilling without meditation. It may bring outer conditions which are enjoyable, but the fulfilment that one gets from inner conditions has more scope. The letting go, the renunciation, brings insight, namely the understanding that the ego is constantly wanting and therefore also wanting to think. When the ego stops wanting, it doesn't need to think. When the ego stops wanting, all unsatisfactoriness vanishes. This is why we should meditate. Now we'll look at the 'how' of meditation.

We're going to employ mindfulness of our in-breath and out-breath. This is ideally experienced at the nostrils. Breath is wind and as it hits the nostrils, there's a feeling. That feeling helps us to focus at this small point. In the beginning it is difficult to do so.

Breath means life and is ideally suited as a meditation subject for several reasons: We always have it with us and can't leave it anywhere else. Yet we take it for granted. We never take a good look at it until we lose it, choke or drown or suffocate. Then all of a sudden breath becomes important. But as long as we have it, we never think of it. Yet it means life, which is the dearest thing each one of us has. It is directly connected with the mind. When one is excited or in a hurry, the breath goes fast. When the mind becomes calm and tranquil, the breath becomes equally soft and tranquil. When the breath becomes so fine we can't find it, that's the moment when we actually enter into a concentrated state. Having the breath as one's meditation subject is the training period for that. It's the only bodily function which is both self-regulating and subject to intention. We can make it deeper, longer or shallower and even stop it altogether for some time.

There are many other methods of paying attention to the breath. We can follow the breath as far in and as far out as we become aware of it. Don't make the breath anything special but just follow its course. This provides a wider base of attention. It is not as exact as keeping the mind at the nostrils and therefore a little easier.

Or you can use breath plus a word, for instance, 'Buddho.' 'Budd' on the in-breath, 'ho' on the out-breath. Breath plus syllable, both together. It's very effective for people to whom 'Buddho' is meaningful.

You can also count one on the in-breath, one on the out-breath, two on the in-breath, two on the out-breath. No less than five, no more than ten. When you reach ten, start at one again. Every time the mind wanders, start at one. In the beginning it doesn't matter if you don't get any further than one.

All minds are alike. You don't have to think: 'I am especially unsuited for this.' Who's 'I' anyway? It's just an untrained mind as opposed to a trained one. Anyone who enters a marathon race can run well and quickly if they have trained for it. It is silly to think 'I'm useless, I can't run fast' if you haven't trained for it.

Counting, or 'Buddho,' or attention at the nostrils, or observation of the breath as far in and out as possible: find which method you feel most comfortable with and then stick to it. If you have practised attention on the rise and fall of the abdomen and you have managed some concentration, then continue with that. Keep your legs in a position you can stay in for some time. The back should be straight but relaxed. Shoulders, stomach and neck should be relaxed. When you find yourself slumping forward, sit up again. The same goes for the head. When you're aware of the head going down bring it back up. Slumping and letting the head fall forward are postures of sleepiness, or at least drowsiness, the very opposite of meditation. Meditation needs total awareness.

You will probably find that the mind just won't stay on the breath no matter what you try, whether it's 'Buddho' or 'one-one, two-two' or whether you concentrate at the nostrils or follow the breath in and out. The mind just will not do it unless you've been practising for some years. The thoughts – the film – will be there. The way to work with that is to quickly label the thought, but if that is too difficult, just call it 'thinking' or 'confusion' or 'remembering,' or even 'planning' or 'nonsense.' It doesn't matter. The minute you give it a label you are stepping back to look at it. Unless you do that you become the thinker and are totally distracted. You are at home worrying about the cat that might have got locked in the bedroom or about the children not getting their proper dinner. Whatever it may be, you're thinking and worrying about it and it's all rationalized in the mind as 'Yes, but I have to think about that.' One doesn't have to think about *anything* when meditating. Life keeps on happening and doesn't need us to think about it. It's constantly arising and ceasing every single moment.

When thoughts arise, look at them, give them a name. Whether it's a correct label or not doesn't matter. Any label during meditation means the thought needs to be dropped. When you have learned to label in meditation, you will be able to label thought as wholesome, profitable, skilful or otherwise in daily living also. When you know it's not skilful or wholesome, you can let go of it. You learn to think what you want to think and when one learns that, one need never be unhappy again. Only a fool becomes voluntarily unhappy.

This is the usefulness of labelling in everyday life but in meditation it means that you have become mindful. This practice is all about mindfulness. The Buddha said: 'The one way for the purification of beings, for the destruction of unsatisfactoriness, for entering the noble path, for realizing freedom from all suffering, is mindfulness.' Knowing 'I'm thinking,' 'I'm not meditating,' 'I'm worrying,' 'I'm anxious,' 'I'm dreaming about the future,' 'I'm hoping, wishing'; knowing only – then back to the breath. If you are having a thousand thoughts, then give them a thousand labels. That is the way to real mindfulness. Knowing the thinking process as well as the contents of the thoughts. These are the foundations of mindfulness in action, the only way to liberation – when actually practised.

Feelings of discomfort will arise because the body is sitting in a position it is not used to, but mainly because we try to keep the body still. The body never likes to be still for any length of time. Even if you have the most expensive mattress and are able to sleep well, the body moves many, many times during the night. It will not stay in the same position because it wants to alleviate its discomfort. The body is uncomfortable and so it moves, even though the mind is only dimly conscious during sleep. When we sit in meditation, the same thing happens. Discomfort arises. Instead of immediately trying to change one's position, which is our habitual, spontaneous, impetuous reaction to pain, to all discomfort that arises, examine the situation. Become aware of the fact of how this has arisen. There is contact with the pillow, the floor or with the other leg. From contact comes feeling. From feeling comes reaction. (This, by the way, is what keeps us in the round of birth and death. Our reactions to our feelings are our passport to rebirth.)

There are only three types of feeling: pleasant, neutral and unpleasant. This one is unpleasant, so the mind says – 'Ah, this is an unpleasant feeling called pain. I don't like it and want to get away from it.' This is how we live every single day of our lives, from morning to night. Whatever feels unpleasant we either run away from or push away, or we try to change the outer cause. Anything to get rid of discomfort. Yet there is no way of getting rid of it until we have also got rid of craving. Whatever we do with our bodies, whichever way we move them, there is sure to be discomfort again, because we're always craving comfort.

Watch the sequence: contact, feeling, reaction. 'This is pain. I want to get away from it.' Instead of trying to get away from it, put your full attention on the spot where the feeling is and become aware of its changing nature. The feeling will either change its location or its intensity. You may be able to become aware that in itself it's moving. It's not solid.

Please become aware of the fact that this body does not *have* suffering, but that it *is* suffering. Only then can we begin to fathom the reality of human suffering. It is not that we have some discomfort sometimes, but that this body consists of suffering. It can't sit or lie still without becoming uncomfortable. Know the impermanence. Know the unsatisfactoriness, which is inherent in the human body. Know the fact that the feeling has arisen without your invitation. So why call it 'mine'? Learn these lessons from the unpleasant feeling and then move, if necessary, but don't move spontaneously. Move only after having examined why you are doing it. Move gently, mindfully without disturbing yourself or your neighbour.

Sitting here, gritting your teeth and thinking 'I'm going to sit here, even though it's terrible. I hate it, but I'm going to do it' only creates a dislike for the whole situation and for meditation. It's just as much a reaction of the wrong kind as moving spontaneously. One is the greed for comfort and the other is the aversion to discomfort. They are two sides of the same coin. The only thing that makes any sense is insight into oneself and one's own reactions, and that brings results. Work with the feelings and thoughts as they arise. Watch both of them being totally impermanent. They arise and disappear, so why do you call them yours? Have you asked them to come? Surely not. You really came to meditate, didn't you? Yet there are all these thoughts. Do they belong to you? Isn't that suffering?

Impermanence, unsatisfactoriness, non-self are the three characteristics to be found in all that exists. Unless we identify them within ourselves, we will never know what the Buddha taught. Meditation is the way to find out. The rest are just words. This is the action.

2 Meditation Affects Our Lives

The cleaning-up process, the purification process I have talked about, takes place in the mind. But you will also find you need to remove some old debris which has accumulated in the body because of our psychological responses.

Imagine a person has been living in a room for the past twenty or thirty years and has never bothered to clean it. All the leftover food, all the dirty clothes, all the rubbish that's accumulated now reaches up to the ceiling. Trying to live amongst that rubbish is extremely unpleasant. But the room's inhabitant doesn't even notice it, until one day a friend comes along and says, 'Why don't you clean up?' So together they clean up a little corner. Then our imaginary person there finds that it's far more comfortable and easier to live in that clean corner. Now they start to clean out the whole room until eventually they can look out of the windows and get a better view and also find room enough to move. Feeling more comfortable, the person can use the mind freely without having to attend to any bodily discomfort.

The house we live in is our body. It doesn't matter how many times we move from town to country, from apartment to home, from home to a room or even from one country to another. We take this body with us until it completely deteriorates, decays and is a heap of bones and then only dust. Until that happens, we carry it along with us wherever we move. It's this house we need to make a little more spacious and at ease.

The psychological accumulation of obstructions and blockages has been deposited by our emotional responses. Mind has put them there so mind can also remove them. In our meditative procedure this means 'knowing the feeling, not reacting, then letting go of it.'

As its second feature, the meditation practice incorporates non-reaction. This is a most important aspect of reaching peace and harmony within ourselves, otherwise our reactions will always be wave motions that overwhelm us and we'll never see the path clearly. It will remain obscure to us. We may hear about it. We may have an inkling what is meant, but we'll never see it ourselves because seeing is 'in-seeing,' the inner vision. This inner vision is obstructed by reactions – our emotional responses.

When we observe feelings and sensations during meditation, there's no need, and usually no inclination, to react. So it *is* possible to abstain from reacting: we're actually doing just that! We can take that non-reaction into daily life with us. Whatever emotion turns up, we can see it as just a feeling which has arisen and which will pass away. If we learn this from our meditation practice we're learning one of the most valuable lessons on how to handle ourselves.

It's a common misconception that because we're alive we know how to live. This is one of our human absurdities. Living life is a skill and most people come a cropper at least once or twice in their lives. They call it a tragedy or 'my' problem. It's just that the skill hasn't been perfected.

The third but equally important aspect of our meditation practice is the personal experience of impermanence. Unless we know it personally, impermanence is going to remain a word only. Words alone can never liberate. The experience is needed. The Buddha's path aims at liberation – complete and total freedom – and this has to be a personal experience. In meditation the experience of impermanence is quite direct: when you attend to your breath, you know that this breath went in and then it went out. It's not the same breath any more. The feeling arises and already it's gone. Then there's a feeling in another spot; such an assortment of feelings and sensations and then there are none left. A pain in the leg, it's moved, it's gone. Feelings come and feelings go.

With a little more meditation skill the impermanence of feeling is easily seen, but we also gain insight into the impermanence of this body of ours. Everybody knows about that. There's no thinking person in the whole world who doesn't know that their body and all other bodies are impermanent.

Yet we all live as if we were permanent and grieve about those bodies that have already submitted to the law of nature, as if it were something unexpected.

This is obviously faulty thinking and doesn't make much sense, does it? It's due to the fact that we close our vision to the realities. We try to look at that which is pleasant. That we are also constantly confronted with the unpleasant is a fact for which we try to blame someone else. Some people go as far as blaming the devil. It doesn't really matter who one blames, whether one's neighbour or the devil. The reality of life is total impermanence and we have to accept and experience it in order to live accordingly.

When we learn to penetrate more deeply we'll become aware that there is constant movement in every cell of the body. We all learned this law of nature in school. We might have been eleven or twelve at the time when we were told that all the cells in the body are renewed every seven years. I distinctly remember trying to figure out whether every cell of the body was going to fall out after seven years and then I'd get a new lot coming back in. Since that didn't seem feasible, I gave up on it. I couldn't figure it out. Now we can understand what is really happening. It means that after seven years all the cells will have deteriorated and been renewed – a constant movement.

Obviously there must be a way of becoming aware of this. With meditative concentration we can become aware of the movement of the skin and under the skin. Then we will have a different outlook on ourselves and on the rest of the world, because now we know with direct knowledge that there is nothing solid or static, least of all this body.

Scientists have proved that there is no single solid building block in the whole of the universe. Everything in existence is made up of energy particles which move so quickly – coming together and falling apart – that they create the illusion of solidity. The Buddha said the same two and a half thousand years ago when he referred to such particles, but he didn't need a laboratory to test and prove it. He experienced it himself. This resulted in his enlightenment. Our scientists know all about it but I dare say they haven't become enlightened. What they must have missed is the personal experience.

We can know for ourselves that there's nothing solid anywhere. Even logic, just plain, intellectual logic, proves that if there were anything solid or static, there couldn't be a human being, there'd be a corpse. But that's just intellectualizing, which isn't enough. It has to be felt. When it's felt in the meditative experience then one knows. What one knows from experience, nobody can dispute. Even if everybody in the world were to say to you 'No. This isn't so. Why don't you think you're solid? Why don't you touch the body? It *is* solid, isn't it?' you wouldn't want to argue or be swayed. When people dispute what the Buddha was teaching, he didn't argue. He wasn't defending a viewpoint. He was talking about his own experience.

With greater concentration and deeper penetration we will notice constant movement in ourselves. The mind realizes that if there's constant movement inside, it must be outside too, so where can any solidity be found? The mind may say 'If there's constant movement, where is the "I"? The feelings have all changed. None are left of a moment ago. The body is moving. There isn't anything I can hang on to. The thoughts are moving, so where am I?' Then, of course, people do find some imaginary possibilities where they can find themselves, such as in a higher self, an essence, a soul, etc. But if that is inquired into a little further it is also shown to be another illusion. Impermanence has to be experienced.

Another aspect of our practice is one of the meditation techniques the Buddha mentions in the discourse on the foundations of mindfulness, the meditation on the four elements: earth, water, fire and air. That feeling of solidity in the body is the earth element. We can also feel the solidity of the meditation cushions we're sitting on. The earth element is everywhere. The earth element is also in water, otherwise we couldn't swim in it or propel a boat over it. The earth element is also in the air. Otherwise birds couldn't fly and neither could an aeroplane.

The fire element – temperature – is in everything too. We can feel it in ourselves if our attention is directed to it. Usually we're only aware of the fire element when we're freezing cold or very hot or think we've got a fever. But temperature is always there. It's in every living being and in all matter.

The water element in us can be felt in the blood, in the saliva, in the urine. The water element is also the binding force. When you have flour and you want to make dough, you have to add water to keep it together. Water is the binding element to be found in everything. Without it all those constantly moving cells would fall apart. There wouldn't be anybody sitting here if we didn't have that binding element to hold us together.

All this is very interesting, isn't it? But it's useless unless it's experienced. Until then it's just another intellectual pastime that one may discuss with friends. Yet, when it is experienced it becomes an inner vision of how things really are. Knowledge and vision of things 'as they really are' is a description frequently used by the Buddha.

We can add space as the fifth element. There are spaces – openings – inside us, in the mouth or in the nose. The interior of the body has open spaces. The universe is space. If we realize this in ourselves and connect to the fact that sameness is found everywhere, we will lose some of our separation technique – 'This is "me" and I'm going to look after "me", the rest of the world may get on as best it can. May the rest of them live long and happily but don't let them come too near.' When we realize that we're nothing but energy particles coming together and falling apart, nothing but the five elements, then what is the 'me' we are so zealously protecting? And what is the rest of the world that seems so threatening?

Meditation is aimed at insight; insight is the goal of Buddhist meditation. The techniques are the tools. You use them in the best possible way. Everybody uses tools a little differently. The more skilful we become with them, the quicker and easier will be the results. But full attention must be on the use of the tool – not the result. Only then will the skill and the ease develop.

3   Calm and Insight

There are many different meditation techniques. In the *Path of Purification* forty of them are mentioned, but there are only two streams, two directions, and these are the two directions one has to take: calm and insight. They work hand in hand. Unless we know the direction we're going, it's highly unlikely that we'll get to our destination. We have to know which way to go.

Both directions, calm and insight, need to be practised in order to obtain the results that meditation can bring. Most people want calm. Everybody's looking for some peace, for that feeling of blissful contentment. If they can get a glimpse of it in meditation, they're quite happy and try to get more of it. With a fair bit of it, many would be contented and satisfied with that alone. But that's not what meditation is designed to do – it's a means to an end. Calm is the means. Insight is the end. The means are essential and necessary but they must never be confused with the end. And yet because it's so entirely pleasant, a new attachment arises.

It is our constant difficulty that we want to keep what is pleasant and reject what is unpleasant. Because we make that our purpose in life, our life really has *no* purpose. It's impossible to get rid of everything unpleasant and to keep everything that's pleasant. As long as we have that as our direction, we have *no* direction. The same applies to meditation.

So how are we going to obtain some calm and what does it actually do for us? By keeping the attention on the breath, there will be some calm eventually. The mind may stop thinking for a moment and will really feel quite at ease. A mind that is thinking is never at ease because thinking is a process of movement and movement has irritation in it. But there may come a moment of ease and we may be able to prolong that moment and as we practise longer there is no reason why we can't do it. It's not that difficult. It may seem difficult in the beginning, but all that is needed is patience, determination, a bit of good kamma (see Chapter 7) and a quiet place.

We must all have a bit of good kamma, otherwise we wouldn't be sitting here. People who make a lot of bad kamma don't usually come to a meditation retreat and if they should come, they don't stay. So the good kamma is already there.

As to patience, we are more or less forced into that by remaining here. One thing you'll have to add to that, the one ingredient needed for this mixture, is determination. When you first sit down make a resolution: 'I'm really going to stay on the breath now, and every time I slip off I'm going to come back.' It's a balancing act, like walking on a tightrope. Each time you slip off you have to bring yourself back onto it. So determination is needed.

When that calm and pleasant feeling arises, which the Buddha called a pleasant abiding, and then it disappears again, which it must, because whatever has arisen will disappear, the first reaction that has to come to mind is knowing the impermanence; not, 'Oh dear, it's gone again' or 'That was nice. How am I going to get it back?' which is the usual way of reacting.

Living according to Dhamma, experiencing according to Dhamma, is an unusual way. It's the other way around from what the crowd does. It's an individual understanding. When the Buddha sat under the Bodhi tree, before his enlightenment, Sujata brought him milk rice in a golden bowl and said he could have the golden bowl also. He threw the bowl into the river behind him and said if it swims upstream against the current, he'd become enlightened. And of course it did. Can a golden bowl swim upstream? What this story means is that when we live according to Dhamma, we have to go against the current of our natural instincts and inclinations. We have to go against what is easy, comfortable and done by everyone. It's much more difficult to go against the stream than to go with the current.

The pleasant abiding, the pleasant feeling, which is first physical then also emotional – first it's pleasure in the body, then it's pleasure and happiness in the emotions, then it can become very, very peaceful – that too has to vanish again. We must see its impermanence and only then are we using this pleasant abiding for a purpose. If we don't see the impermanence, we are using it only for our own comfort. What we are using for our own comfort is self-directed and not directed to losing self, which is the essence of the Buddha's teachings.

The whole of the Buddha's teaching is directed towards losing self. He said, 'There is only one thing I teach and that is suffering and its end to reach.' But that doesn't mean that suffering in the world is going to stop. It means that if there's nobody here to react to suffering there is no suffering. Self will stop. If there's nobody here to have a problem, how can there be a problem? Having pleasant abiding for one's own comfort, one goes in the wrong direction.

Going back to the breath again and again will lead us towards the attainment of calm. The eighth step on the Noble Eightfold Path, right concentration, means meditative absorption. Trying to stay on the breath goes in that direction, but nobody goes into the meditative absorptions by wishing to do so or by just sitting down in meditation once or twice. It takes time. So all that arises while trying to stay on the breath needs to be used for insight. Any thought that arises is not a bothersome intruder, nor an indication that one isn't suitable for meditation, nor that it's too hot or too cold or too uncomfortable or too late or too early – none of that. Thought is not an intruder trying to bother us. It's a teacher to teach us. In the last analysis we are all our own teachers and our own pupils and that is as it should be. But we need to know what to look at in order to be taught by it.

Each thought is a teacher. First of all it teaches us about the unruliness of our mind, that our mind is not reliable and dependable. It thinks thoughts we don't even want to think, when we would much rather be totally calm and collected. The first thing we can learn about our mind is that it isn't such a wonderful part of us as we might have imagined just because we have learned, can remember and understand certain facts and concepts. It is an unruly, unreliable mind, not doing what we want it to do.

The second thing to understand is that we don't have to

believe our mind. We don't have to believe all these thoughts that come up. They have come without our invitation and they'll go away again by themselves. They have little purpose, especially during meditation. Some of them might be twenty years old. Some of them might be pure fantasy. Some might be rather unpleasant and some might be dreams. Some might be like will-o'-the-wisps that won't even appear properly. They all come so quickly that there's hardly time to label them. So why believe all the stuff that one usually thinks?

In meditation we have the opportunity to get to know the mind – the thinking that's going on – and learn not to get involved in it. Likewise why should we believe and get involved in all that thinking that occurs in everyday life? We believe it when our mind says, 'This man is awful' or 'This woman is a liar.' We believe it when our mind says 'I'm so frustrated. I'm so bored' or 'I have to get that thing' or 'I have to go to that place.' We believe it all – but why should we? It's exactly the same process in meditation. Thoughts arise, stay a moment and cease again with no rhyme or reason.

The first time we can really grasp this we'll actually be able to change a thought that's in the mind to one that we would like to have. That's what can be done when we don't believe what the mind says any longer, but just observe its thought processes. It's the same with this air around us. We don't grab hold of it and say it's mine, and yet if it wasn't there we couldn't live. It's just there. Thoughts are like that. The thinking process is natural to the mind and because we are alive the thinking process goes on and on, but it's neither reliable nor believable. On the contrary, most of the thoughts it produces would be much better dropped.

There is something else we can learn about our mind. When we sit in meditation and the concentration doesn't happen but the thinking does, when we feel drowsy or there is lack of attention, then we can learn this about ourselves: that without having some entertainment in the mind, we go to sleep. The mind wants to be entertained. It wants to read a book, watch television, visit the neighbours, do some work, anything to be occupied and entertained. It cannot be happy and contented just on its own. This is an interesting new bit of understanding about oneself.

Imagine being in an empty room by yourself for a week, just you. People consider this dreadful punishment, and it is, because the mind can't handle it. It wants to be fed all the time. Just as the body wants to be fed, the mind does too. It needs input because it's not content with itself. This is another important new revelation about ourselves which we get when we sit in meditation.

Thoughts are very impermanent. They arise and they go. They don't stay, just like the breath. If you pay good attention you may be able to notice their arising. You certainly notice their vanishing, that is easy to see, the arising is a little more difficult. But you can't keep any of those thoughts, can you? They are gone, aren't they? All the thoughts that you have had during the past hour, all have disappeared, haven't they?

Impermanence and non-ownership: you don't really want to own all these thoughts, do you? They're not really worth it, are they? There are hardly any that would be worthwhile, so why try to own them? Why try to think this is me? Why not see that they are just a natural arising and vanishing, that is all. Similarly, with this body – is it really me? It's a natural arising through conception and vanishing through death, a law of nature, a fact of nature, which our ego conceit does not allow us to grasp.

Ego conceit does not necessarily mean that we are conceited people. Ego conceit means that we are not enlightened. Conceit has been eliminated only in Arahants. It means that we are seeing the world and ourselves from the standpoint of 'me' and when we do, the world is often threatening and so are other people because 'me' is fragile and can be easily hurt and toppled.

All our thoughts that arise in meditation will give us an insight into ourselves, into the impermanence of this phenomenon, of body and mind, into the non-ownership of it. If we really owned our thoughts why wouldn't we own something which was worth having? Nobody likes to own rubbish. All of us try to make our possessions worthwhile. In meditation the thoughts are found to be not worthwhile.

The third aspect we can learn from all that thinking is that this is dukkha or unsatisfactoriness. Dukkha doesn't only mean suffering. Dukkha also means unsatisfactoriness, which is a much wider term and embraces everything we experience, even the pleasantest thing because of its impermanence. The unsatisfactoriness of our thinking process becomes very, very clear during meditation, because we actually want to concentrate and yet here we are sitting and thinking.

We gain insight into impermanence, unsatisfactoriness and non-self through personal experience. Nobody knows these three unless they have seen them for themselves. They are very nice words, which most of you may be familiar with, but you need to realize them through direct inner knowledge. Although we experience them every single moment, we're not usually paying enough attention.

We are also dying every single moment, but we don't pay attention to that either. It takes precise mindfulness, which we are trying to learn through the meditation process. Look carefully and see the unsatisfactoriness of the thinking process as its inherent quality.

We can all experience reality – the way things really are – if we expand our awareness to the point where we can actually see it. We are experiencing exactly what the Buddha talked about, but we have to penetrate its meaning. It's no use sitting there and thinking, 'I wish I wasn't thinking' or 'I wish I could concentrate' or 'I wish it wasn't so difficult' or 'I wish my right leg wouldn't hurt so much.' Those are dreams. Those are hopes. We can't afford to dream and hope if we want to get to the bottom of what ails us.

The Buddha said that we are all sick and that the Dhamma is the medicine. He was sometimes called the Great Physician. But just as with any medicine, it is of no use knowing about it or merely reading the label. Reading the label is what's been done for so many thousands of years now. Let's stop reading the label and swallow the pill. It's not so difficult once we know the difference.

When unpleasant feelings arise from sitting in one position the mind immediately rejects and resists that. The mind immediately says, 'I don't like it. This is most unpleasant. I'm not going to last ten days. I need a chair.' or 'Why sit like this? It's silly' or 'It's not worth it. Meditation can't be worth all this discomfort,' or whatever else the mind tries to tell us. It has the ability to tell us anything. It can talk about any subject and it can see any side of the subject. It's an accepted debating technique to talk first about the advantages of a subject and then turn around and debate its contrary aspects. Any mind can do it. Our minds can slip this way and that.

Don't sit there and think, 'I don't like this, my right leg or my back or my neck' – or whatever it may be – 'is very uncomfortable.' *No.* Use the arising of feeling as another way to insight. Feeling is our basis for living. The way we react comes through the contact we make through our senses. We see, we hear, we taste, we smell, we touch and, of course, we also think. (The Buddha talked about the mind, the thinking process, as the sixth sense. We also sometimes refer to our thoughts as a sixth sense.) If we were blind, for instance, the world would appear differently to us. If we were deaf our world would be different again. The same with all the other senses. But here we have all our senses intact, we are making contact through them and from it there come feelings. That cannot be helped. We can't help but make contact. An Arahant also has feelings – three kinds either pleasant, unpleasant or neutral. Everybody has them. The neutral ones are those we are not aware of because we're not attentive enough. We haven't got enough mindfulness yet. But we are certainly aware of the pleasant feelings and we revel in them and try to devise ways and means of keeping them. The whole economy of this globe of ours is geared towards creating pleasant feelings and making people want more of them. If everybody were to reject this, most of the economy would collapse. Pleasant feelings are induced by fans, refrigerators, hot water, cold water, different kinds of food, better mattresses and all the rest of it.

Feelings, everybody has them – pleasant, unpleasant, neutral. They arise in quick succession. Most people spend their life trying to hold on to the pleasant feelings and get rid of the unpleasant ones. We are fighting a lost cause. It's impossible. Nobody can keep the pleasant feelings. Nobody can permanently get rid of the unpleasant ones. As one gets older – as some of you may have noticed – the body has more unpleasant feelings than it used to have. Nobody is exempt. It's the law of nature. Death is certain and very often connected with very unpleasant feelings. But these unpleasant feelings are not confined to old age and death. The youngest, strongest people have unpleasant physical feelings and unpleasant emotional feelings.

If we resolve to keep still for a moment, finally to take a look, to no longer run away from the unpleasant and no longer grasp at the pleasant – maybe for just one meditation session – we will have learned an enormous amount about ourselves. Watching the unpleasant feelings which arise while sitting – and for most people this happens – is another way to insight into one's own reactions. One wants to change the feeling, wants to get away from it. There is a spontaneous, impetuous reaction to the unpleasant feeling by moving to get rid of it as quickly as possible.

In daily living, we try to get rid of unpleasant feelings by getting rid of the people who trigger them in us, by trying to get rid of situations, by blaming others instead of looking at the feeling and saying, 'So, it has arisen. It will stay awhile and it will pass again. Nothing remains the same. If I watch it closely enough I'm using mindfulness rather than reaction.'

This reaction of ours, trying to keep the pleasant and trying to get rid of the unpleasant, is the reason for our continual roaming around the realm of birth and death because there's no direction to it. It's a circular movement. We can't get out that way. It is a merry-go-round. It doesn't have a doorway. We go around and around and around trying to keep the pleasant, trying to get rid of the unpleasant, a never-ending circle. The only opening leading out of that merry-go-round is to look at the feeling and not to react. If we learn that in meditation, even for one moment, we can repeat it in daily living to great advantage.

Everybody has some unpleasant experiences in their lives. People say things we don't want to hear. People do things we don't want them to do. People don't appreciate us, love us, praise us. People go away when we want them to stay. People stay when we would like them to go away. It happens to everyone. The Buddha himself was abused. The Buddha experienced situations that created unpleasant feelings, but he didn't react.

There is only attention to the feeling. So when an unpleasant feeling arises in the body because of sitting still for longer than usual, don't blame anything or anyone. There's no one to blame for the feelings that arise. These are just feelings that arise and cease. Watch the feeling and know. Unless you stand back and look at an unpleasant feeling and not dislike it you will never be able to effect a change. It has to be done once somewhere along the line. This is the ideal situation, to know that the unpleasant feelings are just feelings. They don't need to be owned because they weren't invited by us. We didn't ask for them. Why do we think they are ours?

Unless we realize what is going on in our mind when these feelings arise, we will fall into our old-established habit patterns over and over again. What we think constantly, what we react to over and over again makes grooves in the mind. Like a muddy driveway on which the car goes back and forth and the ruts get deeper and deeper, the same thing happens in our mind. The ruts get deeper and deeper until in the end they become so deep it seems impossible to move out of the ruts and to go forward.

Here is the right situation, here is an occasion, an opportunity to look at the reaction in one's mind towards unpleasant feelings. Not rationalize – 'It's bad for me, my blood circulation, I shouldn't do it, the doctor always says' – nothing like that. Just watch the reaction in the mind. The mind is clever and manipulative. It can do anything. We call it a magician, which is a good word for it. It can pull a rabbit out of any hat. It can rationalize to the point where we are always right and everybody else is wrong.

This is something we must learn through meditation – that it is impossible to be absolutely right. Most of the time all we are doing is defending a viewpoint, which is based on our own ego. Because we have this ego, the 'me' delusion, all our viewpoints, all our opinions are coloured by that. They can't be anything else. It's impossible. If there is a red tinge on the window everything on the outside looks red.

When we get to know our mind and its reactions through the meditative process, we can be more accepting of the fact that while we're thinking one thing, four billion other people are thinking something else. How could it be possible that we are right and the other four billion are wrong? We are defending a viewpoint, which may at times have validity, but only to the point where it relates to ourselves. The only one who can be totally, completely right is an Arahant, who does not have the ego delusion.

All these steps are ways to gain insight, to be used not while the mind stays on the breath but while it is reacting to feelings or thinking. Every moment can be used to gain insight and from that calm arises. A bit of insight creates a bit of calm. When we see that we don't need to pay any attention to our thoughts, it becomes easier to drop them. When we see that we don't have to react to feelings, it is much easier to drop the reaction. A bit of calm also creates a bit of insight and both have to be used.

The teaching of the Buddha goes against the current of our own instincts and is not easy to understand. The mind which can grasp it is a mind which has been trained. Ordinary minds usually argue about it – it's just another pastime, it doesn't have any results. To actually experience inside oneself what the Buddha talked about needs a mind that has become calmer and more concentrated than usual, and has seen itself for what it is, just arising and passing phenomena.

All this can happen while sitting here and trying to watch the breath.

Calm and insight. Insight is the goal. Calm is the means. As long as there is no calm in the mind, there are waves, waves of like and dislike. The waves obscure our vision. One cannot see one's likeness in a pond in which waves are rising high. The water has to become smooth and calm. Likewise the mind has to become smooth and calm and then the vision which arises is clear. We can see with clarity and penetration.

Walking meditation is going in exactly the same direction. As we really become mindful and stay on the movement, calm arises. If the thinking process is there, we use it in order to know what goes on in our mind.

The labelling is another way to know what one's mind is doing and if we can label in meditation, we can label in daily living. Any person of goodwill would drop a thought labelled 'greed' or 'hate.' This is the way to purification. Calmness of the mind is dependent upon purification. Purification arises also through insight, through knowing oneself. Labelling shows us what is going on in the mind. In meditation all labels, all thoughts need to be dropped. In daily living it is the unprofitable, unskilful thoughts that have to go. Once we learn to do that, purification can take place.

The path of purification leads to the end of all suffering.

4 *Four Friends*

We have four friends in our hearts waiting to do our bidding. But we also have five enemies sitting there waiting to jump out at any given moment. They are never at rest (see Chapter 5). The problem is that we are not diligent enough to throw out the enemies and only cultivate our friends. To cultivate one's friends is a natural and sensible thing to do. Yet there is a lack of clarity in people's minds as to how to judge this in themselves.

Our friends are the four divine abidings: loving-kindness, compassion, joy with others and equanimity. These have to be searched for in our own hearts. When we find them lacking in ourselves and know this is to our own detriment, we begin doing something about their development.

LOVING-KINDNESS

Words are dangerous. They give an illusion of permanence. We are fed with words but they are nothing but concepts. They are not real. Imagine a river: the word 'river' can't proclaim the reality of flowing water. The word 'river' is static: the essential quality of a river is that it flows. Loving-kindness can never exist unless it flows from the heart. As long as it's just embedded in a word it is nothing, it is worthless. It doesn't mean anything on its own in the same way that the word 'river' is only a description which one has to experience in order to know it. If you tell a small child 'river' it won't know what you are talking about. But if you put the child's hand in the water and let it feel the flow then the child knows what a river is, whether it is familiar with the word or not.

The same goes for loving-kindness. The word is meaningless. Only when you feel it flowing from your own heart will you get an idea what the Buddha talked about in so many discourses. Life cannot be lived fully unless it's lived with both heart and mind. If one lives with one's heart only, one is prone to emotionalism, a very common error, not strictly confined to females but very much practised by them. Emotionalism means reacting to everything, and that doesn't work. The mind has its rightful place. One has also to understand what is happening. Yet if one only understands well, one may be intellectually advanced, but the heart is not engaged. Both must go hand in hand – heart and mind together. One has to understand and one has to use one's emotions positively, emotions which are fulfilling and bring a feeling of peacefulness and harmony to one's own heart.

Loving-kindness or love – whichever word has meaning for you – is not an emotion resulting from the presence of a lovable person, or because one is with one's family or children, or because somebody is worthy of love. That utilitarian and instinctive reaction has nothing to do with this kind of love. Practically everybody can react in that way. It's not very difficult to love one's own children. Most people manage. It is also not terribly difficult to love one's own parents. Some people can't even do that, though most people manage. But that's not the meaning of mettā or loving-kindness.

When the Buddha talks about loving-kindness he talks about a quality of the heart which makes no distincion between any living being. The highest aspiration mentioned in the loving-kindness discourse (see Chapter 8) is that one should love all beings just as a mother loves her only child. Those of you with children know the feeling you have for your children and can tell the difference. How do you feel about your own children and how do you feel about other people? That is the work one has to do. Unless one is willing to purify oneself until all beings are considered as though one's own children, one hasn't understood loving-kindness and its importance.

If you see a small child who has fallen off a bicycle and is crying, it will be natural to pick it up and console it. That's loving-kindness but not very difficult. The difficulty lies in generating that feeling in one's heart towards everyone, most

of whom are not terrible lovable. None of us is perfectly lovable. Only an Arahant is. Since we ourselves are not perfectly
lovable, why do we expect it of others? Why do we make
such distinctions between those we care to love and those we
don't love? We think we are justified in not loving those who
are not acting in a way we consider proper. Nobody acts in
the right way all the time, including each one of us. If you
give it a moment's thought, we have all made mistakes in our
lives. Even though I don't know your lives, I can be quite
sure by looking at my own. Everybody has made mistakes,
so why expect others to be perfect if we can't do it ourselves?

There are three grades, so to speak, of loving-kindness.
The first one we might call goodwill. We have goodwill towards each other. It is the primary requirement for living
together. If we did not have goodwill for each other we
couldn't even meditate together. We would get up and walk
about. We would make a noise when everybody was quiet.
No country can exist if people don't have goodwill for each
other. Have you ever considered how dependent we all are
on one another? We are dependent upon the postman to
deliver letters, upon the vegetable and fruit seller and the rice
farmer for our food, the municipal government for water. We
are dependent upon the goodwill of our neighbours. Because
goodwill is an essential requirement for survival all manage
it most of the time. When it breaks down, we have chaos.

The next grade of loving-kindness we might call friendship.
We feel friendly towards a certain group of people – our
friends, our neighbours, people we know or someone who
does us a favour. Friendliness is a step towards loving-kindness but it isn't real loving-kindness yet. It is a quality which
is endearing to the heart and endears other people to us. But
it has the near-enemy of love embedded in it, namely affection.
Although we think of affection as something positive, it has
attachment in it. Attachment to our friends and associates, to
those who help us, to those who live with us. That attachment
creates hate, not towards the people we are attached to, but
towards the idea that they might be lost. There is fear and
we can only fear what we hate. Therefore the purity of love
is lost. The attachment makes it impure and thus less satisfying. No total fulfilment can be found. This is what happens

within the family. That is why there is always unsatisfactoriness in that kind of love.

The love one has for one's family can be used as a seedbed to experience the feeling of lovingness. Then one can cultivate it, make it grow, spread it further. Only then does family love have its proper significance. Otherwise it becomes a hotbed of emotions – as it so often is – like a boiling kettle with the lid on. The loving feeling in the family must be used to cultivate that true feeling of loving-kindness in one's heart, which is not dependent on conditions, such as 'my husband, my wife, my daughter, my son, my uncle, my aunt, my mother, my father.' That is all 'my-making and mine-making.' Unless we can transcend that and grow into unconditioned love, the family love has not been used for its full purpose. It has been used for ego support and survival instead. Since survival is a lost cause, it doesn't need our effort. Atom bomb or not, we are not going to survive. There is only one place where we are all going to, where we will all meet.

Our friendships are beset with the same difficulty – namely attachment. We are attached to our friends. We don't want to lose them. We are nice to them so that they will remain our friends. If they are not equally nice back to us, we immediately consider whether we should remain friends. We want the same friendship back, the same consideration and care. It turns into a commercial enterprise. I give something and I want the same value back. This is what most people do so naturally that we don't even think about it. It happens with our friends, but even more so with our loved ones. If they don't love us back, we feel bereft, desolate, depressed. If they should leave, then love seems to be lost. Isn't it absurd that love should be embedded in one other person, or two or three?

Love cannot be encased in a person. A person is nothing but a bag of bones with thirty-two parts in it surrounded by skin (see page 62). How can love be embedded in that? Yet that is what the famous tragedies are all about. *Romeo and Juliet* or *Gone with the Wind* are dramas about someone leaving, someone not being interested, about separation through death. People are bound to leave, either through death or through changing their mind and their feelings. Whether they ought to or not is not the question. How can love be embedded in one or two such persons?

Love is embedded in a feeling. If one hasn't used family love in order to expand and enlarge this feeling then one is bound to experience a trauma when one's attachment disappears for some reason. The primary purpose of family love is getting to know the loving feeling and then working with it.

Working with it isn't confined to a ten-day meditation course nor when one chants the loving-kindness discourse. Neither mind nor heart can be turned on and off like light switches. They need systematic training with patience and determination.

The heart needs training because by nature it isn't constituted to always feel loving-kindness. By nature it contains both love and hate. It contains ill-will, rejection, resentment and fear and also lovingness. But unless we diminish the hate and enlarge the love by doing something about it in our daily life we have no chance of experiencing that peaceful feeling which loving-kindness generates in the heart.

Having love in one's heart – unconditional love for others – creates security in the heart. One knows how one is going to react. One can rely on oneself. One is totally reliable, having no fear. One knows that one is trained to the point where there isn't going to be any reaction of hate or anger, not even a little, to mar one's peacefulness. That is the first and foremost great result of having cultivated loving-kindness in one's heart.

Love is most importantly cultivated when we confront someone who is totally unlovable. That's the time when we can really do the work of changing heart and mind. We are forced to it. Most of us know someone who is difficult to love. We should be grateful for that. In retrospect it is easy to be grateful, but when we confront that person, all the negative sides arise in the heart: dislike, hate, justification for our dislike and hate, rationalization, anger. The time to be loving is when all the negative feelings arise. It is the best time for it.

It is a great pity to have such an opportunity and not make use of it. If you have nobody unlovable in your life right now, use everybody. Every living being is a learning situation for lovingness, no matter who they are, what they do, what they believe. It doesn't matter what they say, whether they are interested in you or whether they have any loving-kindness themselves. None of that counts. The only thing that matters is one's own heart and that is the one thing to remember. 'If my heart can become loving and accepting, if I can cause my heart to have no anger, no resentment, then I have taken a great step on the Dhamma path.' The Dhamma has to be understood, digested and lived.

Everyone has the opportunity to work on their responses to others. Everybody meets people all the time and always there are some who do not agree with them. If one clamps one's mouth shut and doesn't say anything, that doesn't create any loving-kindness. All it creates is resentment, suppression, worry, or it may result in indifference. None of that is helpful or purifying. The great result of being reliable and secure within oneself can only come when one knows one is going to respond in the fullness of one's heart.

The Buddha spoke about eleven benefits that come from loving-kindness. The first three are: 'One goes to sleep happily, one dreams no evil dreams, and one wakes happily.' If anybody has difficulty falling asleep, you can be sure it is because of a lack of loving-kindness, and sleeping pills don't answer this problem. Lovingness does. Then the subconscious also doesn't act in an unpleasant way so there are no evil dreams, no nightmares and one wakes with the same feeling that one had on going to bed, namely the same loving thoughts towards all beings, as one had the previous day.

It's useful to make a balance sheet at night. It can be just in the mind, but it can also be in writing if you are inclined that way. Make a balance sheet: 'How often have I felt lovingness towards another person today?' On the other side of the sheet put: 'How often have I felt anger, hurt, resentment, rejection, fear, anxiety today, when confronting other people?' Then total it up and if the balance is on the debit side, make a resolution to change it. Every good shopkeeper makes a balance sheet at the end of the day and if his merchandise doesn't have good customer acceptance, obviously he will change it.

It's a skill. It's not an inbred character fault or ability. It's a skill to change oneself again and again until all impurities

have been cleansed. It's not because other people are so lovable. They're not. If they were, they'd be roaming around in
the god realms. They wouldn't be down here. This is the fifth
realm from the bottom in a cosmology of thirty-one realms.
If we are in class five from the bottom and thirty-one exist
altogether, well, what can you expect?

There is a lot to learn in this realm and that is its purpose.
It is a continual adult education class, that is what this whole
human realm is designed for. Not for the purpose of finding
some comfort, not in order to have riches, wealth, possessions. Not to become famous or to change the world. People
have many ideas. Life is strictly an adult education class and
this is the most important lesson, namely to cultivate and
make the heart grow. There is no lesson more important. Just
as in a garden, when weeds surround a beautiful rose bush.
First of all its nourishment is taken away and it can't flourish
and then nobody can enjoy the flowers or their fragrance.
Eventually the weeds will smother the roses. The same happens within our heart. The rosebush is our lovingness which
is growing there. If we don't cut down the weeds and make
sure that the flowers can be seen and the fragrance experienced – if we don't get these weeds down to manageable size,
but let them grow and grow – they will eventually smother
loving-kindness altogether. The weeds are anger and all its
associated emotions.

Most people are looking for someone to love them. Some
people find a few to love them and then might be able to love
back. But some people are unfortunate and cannot find anyone. They become bitter and resentful. Yet really it works
exactly the other way around. If we ourselves are loving, then
there are innumerable people around, because everybody
wants to be loved. That someone loves us doesn't mean that
we are loving. The other person is feeling the love. We don't
feel a thing. All we feel is gratification that somebody has
found us lovable. That is another ego support, to make the
ego bigger. But loving others goes in the direction of making
the ego smaller.

The more love we can extend, the more people we can
include in it, and the more love we have. Whatever we can
generate, that much we have within us. It is a very simple

equation but few people see it that way. Everybody is looking for more people to love them. It doesn't work. It's absurd, but we have so many absurdities in our lives.

This is in line with another one of our eleven benefits spoken of by the Buddha: 'One is beloved by humans and by nonhumans.' If we extend love towards others they'll feel attracted to us. There's no scarcity of people to love us. We give them love not because we want to give something, not because they need it, not because they are worthy of it, but because the heart has been trained to do nothing else. It is just like being trained in arithmetic. If a set of figures is put in front of you, you will be able to add them up. What else should you do with them if you want to know their total? Your mind has been trained in that way. If the heart has been trained, it extends love no matter what happens.

'The devas protect one.' Devas are beings of higher realms, guardian angels. A person who extends love to others is protected. Often people will object: 'If people are nasty to you and you respond with lovingness, won't they think you weak and take advantage of you?' If they do – which is quite possible because people are inclined that way – that's their bad kamma, isn't it? But the person with the lovingness will never lose. How can you lose the love you carry around in your own heart? If somebody takes advantage of you, it is another instance of learning whether your heart has already been trained – whether you have any resentment or whether you can actually love that person and respond with kindness. It is another instance where we can check whether we're doing the necessary work. Of course love includes consideration of other people's rights. A person who takes advantage lacks love. The weakness which one may be afraid of showing is a fallacy because love gives strength not weakness. A person who has nothing but loving feelings feels safe and secure, totally at ease because nothing can sway them. Love strengthens, not weakens. But if it is coupled with passion as it is often misunderstood to be, then it weakens one because it has created dependency. If it's a feeling and a cultivation of one's own heart, then it is as strong as a rock. The protection that one gets is a protection through one's own purity.

'One's mind is quickly concentrated' is another one of the

eleven benefits of loving-kindness. That's the reason for starting every meditation session with loving thoughts for yourself. The mind cannot concentrate without the three foundations of generosity, moral conduct and loving-kindness. These
are the three pillars of meditation, which support meditation
practice. Loving-kindness, as a feeling in one's heart, is an
absolute essential for concentration because it creates peace
and calmness in the mind. If that's lacking, more loving-kindness meditation at the beginning of each session may be helpful in order to cultivate lovingness within yourself.

Loving others cannot happen if one doesn't love oneself.
But loving oneself does not mean indulging oneself. Always
wanting it nice and comfortable, not a single mosquito around,
or always the kind of food one is used to. That is indulgence
not love. That's being silly. The love a mother has for her
child is permeated with wisdom. If the mother indulges the
child, the child is going to pay for it dearly and so is the
mother. But if the mother loves truly, she won't spoil her
child. She will bring her child up with love and wisdom and
– because of her love – demand adherence to certain standards
of behaviour. This is what we have to do with ourselves. We
have to demand compliance with certain rules of conduct
from ourselves because we love ourselves. Coming to a meditation course and sitting through it is loving oneself.

The concentration that everybody would like to reach in
meditation is truly dependent upon lovingness in the heart.
It is also dependent upon practice. But if practice is lacking,
loving-kindness can take its place in making concentration
happen.

'One has a shiny complexion.' This means one has a pleasant expression on one's face. It's a far better beauty aid than
anything one can buy at the chemist. That's where real beauty
comes from, and if one wants to be reborn beautiful this is
the ingredient. A young person may look beautiful without
having much inside. But one can often see the real beauty of
a person by observing them. The Buddha was often described
as making such an impression on people, just by walking
along the street, that they followed him and became his disciples after only seeing him once. In one instance Rahula, his
son, became proud about looking beautiful like his father.

The Buddha immediately reproved him and said, 'All form should be regarded thus: this is not mine, this I am not, this is substanceless.'

Another of the eleven benefits is that 'Fire, poison and arrows won't hurt one.' People don't throw arrows much these days but they do use guns or clubs: fire and poison are still used for aggression. This doesn't necessarily mean that one is invincible, but it does mean that persons with a great deal of lovingness don't usually find themselves in situations such as that. But if they do, their heart is not affected. Their possessions, maybe, but not their heart. One is invincible in the heart because one is no longer able to hate.

'One dies an unconfused death.' We are all going to die. The moment of death is important, because it is the moment of rebirth, it's actually our birthday. Everybody talks about death as something sad and filled with grief. If death is experienced consciously, with awareness and full loving-kindness, then it is a good birthday. That's all it really is unless one is an Arahant. Our habitual way of thinking and feeling will be with us at the end of life, at the moment of death. The habitual thinking pattern cannot be changed suddenly. If it has been one of loving-kindness, there will be awareness, no fear, peace and security in the heart. The instant of death needs to be a profitable moment because it's the start of a whole new lifetime again.

Loving-kindness can be cultivated in the heart with great benefit to ourselves. Someone once said, quite rightly, 'That's an ego-trip.' It is. As long as we have an ego, every trip we're on is an ego-trip. But at least this is one trip in the right direction. This journey goes towards the ultimate destination – egolessness – because the more loving-kindness there is in the heart, the less ego. The more the ego diminishes, the more love can come from the heart. When other people are taken into the heart the self has to step aside to make room. Others are benefiting by that as a matter of course, but that is a secondary consideration. The only person we can lead to liberation is ourself. Everybody has to go alone, solitarily. Anybody who would like to come along is welcome. The band-wagon is big and there aren't enough people on it yet.

COMPASSION

Our second friend is compassion. Its far-enemy is cruelty. Its near-enemy is pity. Pity is called a near-enemy beause it seems so similar. It is very close and yet it is an enemy. Pity arises when we are sorry *for* someone. Compassion is when we are sorry *with* someone. 'Com' means with, 'passion' is strong feeling. Compassion is empathy – to feel with another person.

Compassion arises when one realizes the suffering, the unsatisfactoriness that exists within oneself. Only then can one feel with another person. Otherwise one is still under the delusion that everything is all right with oneself, that it's only other people who are having a bad time. If one sees clearly within oneself all the unsatisfactory states that arise constantly in quick succession – the likes and dislikes, the regrets and the resentments, the fears and the worries, the tensions – then one knows that everyone is subject to the same. Then when someone else is having a difficult time one can feel with that person, because one knows about one's own problems.

Compassion can be an excellent starting point for love. If one can arouse in oneself a genuine feeling for another person, realizing how difficult the situation must be for them, what may be happening, then from there it's not such a far cry to having a feeling of lovingness towards that person.

But again, we mustn't discriminate between people and that is what mostly happens. We can usually feel some compassion for those with whom we have some affinity. They belong to the same group or to the same religion, the same country, the same neighbourhood or the same club – whatever it is that we are interested in. Something that we can call 'mine,' which makes it selective. That selection is what separates us from each other and wherever one goes in the world this separation exists. This creates all the strife between people.

The separation from each other is based on our ego concept. This is 'me' and I've got to protect 'me' and defend 'me.' 'Me' feels threatened. 'Me' feels threatened so often that one doesn't even know 'me' very well. One doesn't know who that 'me' really is. All one is aware of is the threat to 'me' with its attendant fear. When there is fear there is no compassion because fear is based on hate. We only fear what we don't like. We don't fear what we love. The more fear there is in the heart, the less compassion. Fear is always based on the ego concept. An Arahant is totally fearless. There is no fear in a person who's enlightened. There is nothing to fear because there's nothing to gain and nothing to lose. It has all become immaterial, without significance. The more ego, the more fear. Fear of the dark, fear of thieves, fear of bad weather, fear of the future, all kinds of fear. Fear is always based on the protection of that illusory 'me.' And the more we want to protect 'me' the less we can have compassion.

Compassion can, of course, be lip-service. We can pretend. Most of us are extremely good at pretending. Once Pessa, an elephant trainer's son, came to see the Buddha and said to him: 'I have no problems with elephants. They do exactly as they appear to want to do. They have an intention and I can see that intention and then they follow through with it. But I have a lot of problems with people. They say one thing and do another.' The Buddha said, 'That's right. The elephant lives in the jungle, but the human being lives in a mental jungle.' People say one thing and mean or do another. The worst of it is that we're not even aware of it. We think that is the way it ought to be done. We think that this is convention, custom or tradition, and we don't thoroughly examine our thoughts, speech or actions.

Only when we examine ourselves with ruthless honesty will we ever know what the Buddha taught. The Buddha talked in depth about what happens with each one of us. Superficially we all look different and seem to have different ideas and intentions. Superficially there seems to be a great difference between people but underlying it all there is a unity. We all are made from the same recipe and we are all searching for the same thing and going to the same destination. The differences we find are arbitrary. They are all based on the ego concept.

Every thinking person bemoans the fact that there is no peace between nations. Everybody would like to see peace on this globe. Obviously there isn't any. In this century there has been a war somewhere practically all the time. Every country has an enormous defence system where a lot of energy, money and manpower is used. This defence system is turned into an attack system the minute anyone makes even the slightest unfriendly remark or seems to be moving towards an invasion of airspace or of territorial waters. This is rationalized and justified with, 'We have to defend the border of our country in order to protect the inhabitants.' Disarmament is a hope and a prayer, but not a reality. And why? Because disarmament has to start in everyone's heart or wholesale disarmament will never happen.

The defence and attack which happens on a large scale happens constantly with us personally. We're constantly defending our self-image. If somebody should look at us sideways or not appreciate or love us enough, or even blame us, that defence turns into an attack. The rationale is that we have to defend this person, 'this country' which is 'me,' in order to protect the inhabitant, 'self.' Because almost every person in the world does that, all nations act accordingly. There is no hope that this will ever change unless every single person changes. Therefore it is up to each of us to work for peace inside ourselves. That can happen if each ego is diminished somewhat, and ego only diminishes when we see with ruthless honesty what's going on inside us.

Labelling thoughts is one way of doing that. One finally finds out what kind of rubbish one is thinking and one has fewer grandiose ideas about one's person and one's thinking capacity. It is one of the aspects of meditation.

Another aspect of ruthless honesty with oneself is to admit when one has unpleasant feelings and cannot handle them. One recognizes that one is constantly in search of sensual gratification. That ruthless honesty makes it possible to diminish the ego a little. When one does that, compassion becomes a possibility – real compassion, not just the word. The words are facile. They are available to anybody who can talk. Small children from the age of six upwards can repeat the loving-kindness discourse (page 96). It all sounds very nice, but what does it do? The repetition of these words cannot possibly bring about a feeling, yet we live according to our feelings. That's why it's so essential to know our own feelings. We believe we live according to our thinking, but we don't.

First comes the feeling and then comes the reaction. Then the thinking process justifies the reaction.

Understanding our feelings is of the utmost importance. It's of the essence. How can we ever know what it means to love or what it means to have compassion if we don't feel it? We may know about it, but how can we ever actualize it, if we don't feel it? Liberation is not 'knowing,' it is 'feeling.' Everybody feels a 'me.' Everybody knows their name, but everybody also feels that the name describes this special 'me.' One can feel the self. So in order to get to non-self, it has to be felt too.

Compassion is a feeling in the heart and does not need special reasons or special conditions. It can be totally *un*conditional. We don't have to wait for special occasions to arise, namely that someone is beset by tragedy or their body gives them great pain. If we have to wait for those to arouse compassion in ourselves, it is going to be an on-and-off affair, probably more off than on. That's not a compassionate heart. A compassionate heart – just like a loving heart – feels compassion all the time because everybody has suffering. It's embedded in the first Noble Truth of the Buddha's teaching. There is nobody without it, because life – existence – *is* suffering. This doesn't mean tragedy. It means that all that happens contains friction and irritation and a constant wish for more, or for remaining so, or for becoming different. Total equanimity is not the lot of human beings, other than Arahants. Compassion is called for at all times, not only when tragedies have befallen people.

This feeling for others is only possible with a diminished ego. Ego-concern is at the root of the problems people have with each other. Because everybody has the same ego-concern, nobody can really feel for another person. Anybody who does, stands out as somebody special. A sad and absurd state of affairs, because compassion and loving-kindness in the heart make the one who has them happy. Yet most people are lacking them. There's very little real happiness to be found anywhere. Yet these two feelings in the heart are sources of joy, because they diminish the ego. Anyone who is only ego-centred has little joyfulness because there is no satisfaction to be had in ego gratification. We can never get to the end of our problems. There's always a new one arising. But when one lets go of that and directs one's attention to the all-prevailing unsatisfactoriness, to which every living being is subject, not only can one see the universality of it, but also that one's own particular suffering has really no significance. It's part of the whole of existence. Then compassion for oneself and all beings arises. And determination to make an end to all suffering gains the strength it needs to succeed.

SYMPATHETIC JOY

The next of our four friends is joy with others or sympathetic joy. The far-enemy of it is envy which is easy to see. The near-enemy is affectation or hypocrisy, saying one thing and meaning another. For example, if someone has some good fortune and one feels obliged to offer congratulations, using just the words but not feeling anything; or worse using the words and thinking the opposite. Something like: 'Why isn't it happening to me? Why always to someone else?'

Joy with others is a sure antidote for depression. Anybody who suffers from depression is suffering from the lack of joy with others, the lack of sympathetic joy. One cannot always have joyful occasions, joyful thoughts in one's own life, but if one has joy with other people one can surely find something to be happy about.

One can also have joy with other people's abilities. Most people find it extremely difficult to admit that someone else is very capable. Reluctantly one sometimes says, 'Well, he can do that, *but*...' and immediately a detraction follows instead of joy with the other person who can do something better than oneself. There are so many things other people can do better than ourselves. Some can sing and some can paint, some can dance and some can translate, some can make money and some can live without. Everybody has some ability. One can find innumerable occasions for being joyful.

Joy with others is also good kamma-making. I was in a little village once where there was a special bell attached to the temple. Whenever anyone in that village had some good fortune, they would go and ring that bell. If the harvest was brought in, or the daughter got married, if someone came back from the hospital, or a good business deal had been arranged, if the roof had been reshingled, anything at all that gave them joy. When the bell was rung everybody would come out, look in the direction of the person who was ringing the bell and say, 'Well done. Well done.' The one who was ringing the bell was making good kamma by making it possible for the others to share his joy. The others were making good kamma by sharing another's joy.

Most villages, towns and cities don't have special bells for that purpose. We have to ring our own bell. This is something of the utmost importance to remember, to remember what the Buddha taught under all circumstances and to actually follow through with it. Not just to remember it on special occasions or when tragedy strikes, but to remember it at all times because it is the recipe for happy and peaceful living. The Buddha said: 'There is only one thing I teach and that is suffering and its end to reach.' He made a gigantic promise and he kept that promise. That's what he teaches – the end of suffering. Unless we remember that ego is at the bottom of the whole problem and try to do something about it, we have forgotten his teachings. They are not an occasional benefit. They need to be inside the heart and mind all the time.

EQUANIMITY

The last of our four friends is the crowning glory of all emotions: equanimity, even-mindedness. Its far-enemy is anxiety and restlessness but its near-enemy is indifference and the two are easily confused. Indifference is a state of mind which says, 'I don't care, as long as it doesn't happen to me or my family. I don't want to know about it. I don't want to get upset.' Indifference is cold, rejecting. It has no love in it, no loving-kindness. We just want to protect ourself, and to accomplish that we become disinterested.

But even-mindedness is based on the wisdom and the insight that everything changes, on an understanding of total impermanence. No matter what happens, it will all come to an end. Whatever may be, it doesn't have any real significance. The 'door to the deathless' through impermanence is the signless door, which means no significance. There is nothing in the whole of the universe that is really significant except liberation. So equanimity derives from the insight that everything constantly changes: whether what has happened feels good or bad is neither a cause for elation nor for depression. It's just happening. We are here as this specific human being for maybe sixty, seventy, eighty years. So what's all the hustle and bustle about? What is there to gain? Where is there to go? It's all just happening.

The only reason we have no true equanimity is because of ego protection. We fear that 'I' may be in some sort of danger, some sort of attack on 'me,' which may make my life less secure. The security that everyone is looking for is a myth anyway. It is an illusion. There is no security. Everybody is subject to death. Everything we have is subject to destruction. Everyone we love is subject to death, decay, disease, disappearance, changing their mind. There is no security in any of that. The lack of equanimity which arises when things happen which we don't like is based on the illusion that we've lost something that is really significant to our well-being. This is our ego-protection. But even our well-being is an illusion because there is nothing that can ever make us truly well and lastingly secure.

Equanimity needs more than just the determination to be even-minded. Determination is useful but it can easily be based on suppression. We tend to suppress our strong emotions. That doesn't benefit us at all, because they come out eventually. What we suppress in one way finds different outlets. Suppression can result in sickness or in depression. It can show itself in other upheavals. We are not upset by one particular situation, but by another one.

Equanimity needs insight. When it is perfectly cultivated it is one of the seven factors of enlightenment. Complete equanimity is a privilege reserved for the Enlightened Ones. Yet unless we practise it now, how will we advance and grow?

Through meditation we *can* begin to see the flux and the flow, how the mind changes constantly. Can anybody remember what they were thinking about ten minutes ago? In the last meditation? In the one before that? Nobody. We can't keep any thought, we can't keep anything. Everything is momentary. Just because we may have had a house or a person around us for the past thirty years doesn't mean we can keep them. Because they have been with us for a long time they appear to be permanent. But we can easily notice in our meditation how our thoughts come and go and never stay with us. What is there to get worried about if everything moves, everything disappears? Constant flux, constant flow.

Only so long as this is happening is there a human being. So long as the breath is moving, the blood pulsating, the thoughts and feelings changing, so long as all the cells in the body are decaying – just so long do we have a human being. When that stops, we have a corpse. Without that flux and flow, we wouldn't be here and yet we try to make that flux and flow permanent. We try to make it solid. 'This is me and I want to make sure that everybody knows this is me. I've got a name and there are certain people and possessions that belong to me. I've got viewpoints and want to make sure everybody knows them.' This is trying to instil permanency into a person. Yet there can only be a person because it is constantly changing and in the end it's going to change into a corpse. Then we can start all over again.

Equanimity will have to be imbued with some basic insights in order to arise. It also has to contain acceptance. So long as there is no acceptance, there is suffering because this implies resistance. The opposite of acceptance is resistance and resistance hurts. If one pushes against something, it hurts one's hand. If one goes along with it there is no pain at all. Acceptance of things the way they are creates equanimity, and equanimity creates security in the heart.

These four emotional states – the divine abidings – create security in the heart. If one cultivates the four friends to some extent, one will feel secure, at peace and at ease because one realizes that the world may condemn and abuse, but one doesn't have to take part in all that. The Buddha said, 'I don't quarrel with the world. The world quarrels with me.' That is the security of equanimity.

5 *Loving-Kindness Meditation*

Please put the attention on the breath for just a moment to become centred.

Take a look into your heart and see whether there is any worry, fear, grief, dislike, resentment, rejection, uneasiness, anxiety. If you find any of those, let them float away like the black clouds that they are...

Then let warmth and friendship arise in your heart for yourself, realizing that you have to be your own best friend. Surround yourself with loving thoughts for yourself and a feeling of contentment within you...

Now surround the person nearest to you in the room with loving thoughts and fill that person with peace and wish for that person's happiness...

Now surround everyone here with loving thoughts...

Let the feeling of peacefulness extend to everyone here, and think of yourself as everyone's good friend...

Think of your parents, whether they are still alive or not. Surround them with love. Fill them with peace and gratitude for what they have done for you, be their good friend...

Think of those people who are nearest and dearest to you. Embrace them with love, fill them with peace as a gift from you, without expecting them to return it to you...

Think of your friends. Open up your heart to them, to show them your friendship, your concern, your love, giving it to them without expecting anything in return...

Think of your neighbours who live near you, the people you meet at work, on the street, in the shops, make them all your friends; let them enter into your heart without any reservation. Show them love...

Think of anyone for whom you have dislike or with whom you may have had an argument, who has made difficulties for you, whom you do not consider your friend. Think of that person with gratitude, as your teacher, teaching you about your own reactions. Let your heart go out to that person because he or she too has difficulties. Forgive and forget. Make him or her your friend...

Think of all those people whose lives are far more difficult than ours, who may be sick, in hospital, who may be in prison, in an orphanage or in war-torn countries, hungry, crippled, blind, without friends or shelter, never able to hear the Dhamma. Open up your heart to all of them. Make them all your friends, show them love, wish them happiness...

Put your attention back on yourself. Feel contentment arising in you from making right effort, happiness which comes from loving and joy which comes from giving. Become aware of these feelings, experience the warmth they create in and around you...

May all beings be happy.

6 Five Hindrances

Most of you have heard of Māra. Some of you don't know his name, but you all know him. He's the tempter. He tempts us into that which is apparently pleasurable. Māra came around when the Buddha was sitting under the Bodhi tree on the verge of enlightenment. Obviously Māra is not some fellow with red flames coming out of his ears, trying to pull us into a hell realm. Māra is the temptation that sits in our own heart. If it's possible for the Buddha just before his enlightenment to be visited by Māra – have temptations arise in his own heart – what to say about us?

The difference is that the Buddha knew that this was Māra, – temptation. He knew and we very often do not. We rationalize and justify. I've seen a sticker on the back of a car which said 'If it feels good, it must be right.' A lot of things could feel good, possibly even killing a person might feel good at the time of doing it.

The temptations that sit in our hearts are our defilements, our underlying tendencies creating havoc again and again. Because we don't like to admit that there is something within us which needs purifying, we justify it in any way we can. Sometimes people say, 'Well, I'm supposed to enjoy myself' or 'This is the way I feel, so I must need it.'

The temptations in our heart are there practically all the time and because we don't recognize them we are often in a quandary. We are being pulled this way and that. For instance, right now: we know it's better to hear Dhamma, but wouldn't it also be nice to go to sleep? If we were left alone, without a lot of people sitting here, it is quite likely we'd wander off to bed.

Māra is there all the time. He is constantly trying to make

us do what's most comfortable and creates more sense pleasures, without admitting that no *real* pleasure can ever come
through the senses because it doesn't last.

The Buddha said that there are five mental states which are
everybody's enemies, the five hindrances. We all have them,
we are all tempted by them. The first two are the worst, with
the heaviest consequences.

SENSUAL DESIRE

The very first enemy is called sensual desire. It's a difficult
one to recognize because it's highly approved of in society.
Every advertisement, television commercial, department store
and shop window is geared towards arousing sensual desire.
Indeed, the more people are able to gratify sensual desires
with bigger cars, newer houses and beautiful clothes, the
more successful they are considered to be. Since the gratification of sensual desire brings momentary pleasure it has the
appearance of being something good. 'If it feels good, it must
be right.' It has that false glitter about it. Nobody blames
anyone for trying to gratify their desires. We don't even know
we are doing it. It's quite amazing to be so unaware of what
one is doing.

This is not the case with the second enemy – ill-will, anger.
It's the other way around. It's constantly being blamed. It
doesn't bring any pleasurable sensations. Everybody tries to
get rid of it. Sometimes of course we try to justify it. 'I had
to get angry because he, she or they acted in an objectionable
way.' But it is not approved of in society and it doesn't create
any pleasurable sensations and therefore one doesn't have
the mistaken notion that it is something good. Anger and ill
will, dislike and resentment, rejection, fear, anxiety, none of
these are pleasurable, and if one gets angry enough, it is
deserving of blame.

Sensual desire creates some pleasure when it is gratified.
Yet it is as much an enemy as anger or ill will. They are two
sides of the same coin. As much as there is one, that much
will there be of the other. Sensual desire creates craving which
is frequently thwarted. Ordinary people can't get all of their
sensual desires gratified. The more of them one has, the more

of them one might find rejected. Then one gets angry that one can't get what one wants. Nobody can have what they want all the time. It's impossible.

These are the two enemies that make difficulties for us in daily living and they also make it very hard to meditate properly. If anybody has been wondering – I dare say some of you have – why concentration is so difficult to achieve, especially if you have just started to meditate, these are the reasons.

Sensual desire is the one that says 'I'd like to sit more comfortably.' Sensual desire is the one that says 'I'd like to go to sleep now.' Sensual desire says, 'I'd really like to talk, I'd really like to have a walk outside. It's too hot. I'd like to have a cold shower. I'm hungry. I want something to eat. I'm thirsty. I must drink. I'm not feeling comfortable, so I can't meditate.' That's sensual desire, and it has something to say most of the time.

It will only stop talking when the meditation experience results in far greater pleasure than sensual gratification can provide. Namely the happiness and tranquillity which come from concentration. Only then does sensual desire disappear for the time of meditation, not permanently by any means, but for that short period.

Because we have our senses, because we are born with them, we want to feed them. Just as we want to feed the body, so we also want to feed the senses. We would become ill otherwise.

Before the first astronauts were sent off, one of the training methods used in America was the sense-deprivation chamber where there was no gravity and so no touch sensation. It was soundproof and there was nothing to see. Everything was grey. Food came through a tube and was tasteless. The astronauts being trained were to ring a bell when they had had enough. I believe that the longest anyone lasted was eight hours.

Food through the senses is necessary to us and we are attached to it. That attachment gives us the illusion that this is the most important thing there is, that this is where our direction lies – seeing beautiful sights, hearing pleasing sounds, tasting good tastes, smelling good scents, having pleasant touch sensations and thinking thoughts which please us.

But that kind of direction in life – and every person who hasn't trained in Dhamma and meditation has it – cannot be successful. Its fool's gold. It glitters but it has no value because it's so short-lived.

Imagine you were to eat an extremely good meal which tasted excellent, and you were to say, 'This is very good.' Your friend would invite you then, 'Well, if it's so good, please, keep on eating. You can stay here and eat from now until tomorrow morning.' What misery, mental and physical. The only way a meal can be enjoyable is if it lasts twenty or twenty-five minutes. On a very hot day you like to take a cool shower. You're enjoying the shower, and so you say, 'Oh, this is nice. Now I feel pleasant and cool.' Then your friend says, 'Well, in that case why don't you stay in the shower for the next five or six hours?' Utter misery, isn't it? Nobody would ever dream of that. Ten minutes, fifteen minutes, maximum.

The same with every other sensual gratification. It's no longer a pleasure when it lasts too long. It becomes misery. Yet it's what the whole world is searching for – momentary sensual gratification. People even get drunk looking for pleasure, which is obviously not a pleasurable sensation once they are drunk. All searches for happiness through the senses that people attempt are doomed to failure.

The senses are nothing but physical manifestations – ears, eyes, nose, palate, body – that have a sense consciousness. There is nothing personal about them, nothing essentially wholesome or unwholesome. There's no good or bad kamma being made through the senses. Bad kamma is made in the mind when we want to keep and renew the sensual pleasure.

Some people get their sense pleasures through activities such as getting drunk or even hurting others, drugs or sex. These are very gross sensual pleasures connected with unwholesomeness. Others can find sensual pleasure in watching wild flowers, sunsets, listening to beautiful music. These are also sensual pleasures, but far more refined.

The misery arises from the fact that we want to own, keep and experience the pleasure again and again. When people see beautiful flowers, the first thing they do is reach out and pluck them. Why not just leave them there for everyone to look at? No. 'I want to own that which is beautiful.'

The enjoyment of the senses becomes more refined when there's more purification in a person. The smallest thing can be enjoyed, but the danger lies in wanting it. This wanting – the craving – brings the unsatisfactoriness because the wanting can never be fully satisfied. We're always lagging behind. There's always something more beautiful to be seen, something more to be heard or touched. There's always something else. This creates much restlessness, because we can never get total satisfaction.

Because we are not fully satisfied inside ourselves we think that the fault lies with the object. There must be something more wonderful to be found. People search the world. It's very easy these days to go around this little globe of ours. All one needs is an air-ticket. People go here and there in search of more excitement, new scenery, new experiences. Collecting experiences has become a fad. This does not satisfy either because the experiences don't last. No experience one has ever had is still here. All gone. All memory. Nothing can be collected. It might be more useful to collect stamps than experiences. At least the stamps can be looked at.

Sensual desire was compared by the Buddha with being in debt. If you have a house and you owe money to the bank on that house, you have to go every month to pay off with interest. But in the case of the house, eventually it might be fully paid for. With sensual desire, there's no such thing as paying off the debt. Sensual desire arises again and again. It's never paid off. We get hungry again. We get thirsty again. We want to see and hear and taste and touch again and again.

The Buddha also compared it to a traveller who has gone on his journey without any provisions. He gets very hungry and thirsty. He sees a village in the distance and gets quite joyful, thinking, 'Oh, there's a village where I can get something to eat and drink.' When he gets to the village, he finds it totally deserted. An empty village. So he has to go on to find another village and again it's deserted.

The hope and anticipation of the gratification of sensual desire is that which makes it pleasurable. Once it has been gratified, it's already finished and done with and a new desire arises.

The Buddha also compared sensual desire with a pond into which many colours have been thrown. The passion of one's desire shows up in the many different shades which cover up the luminosity of one's mind. This is our difficulty. Because we are beset with desire, we can no longer see that there could be something else much more important. We only see the desire and we only see the possibility of its gratification. We cannot recognise ourselves any more.

The Buddha gave several antidotes for this. The most important antidote is, first of all, to understand that sensual desire is an enemy which wrecks our inner household, creates fear that we may not get what we want and enmity towards those who are getting what we want – envy, jealousy – states of mind which are so unpleasant, yet cannot arise unless we want what another person has. It's the only way these feelings can arise.

It's essential that one understands that this is the cause of our human problems: wanting the pleasurable sensations, wanting the comfort, wanting the gratification, often not getting them and never being able to keep them. Letting go of wanting means letting go of dissatisfaction. But it isn't possible to do that overnight or just by talking or reading about it. It's a gradual process. The first step is to sit with an uncomfortable sensation. Not wriggling and shifting around, not trying to get out of this discomfort by changing position. There is no wriggling out of suffering. Suffering cannot be eliminated in this way. The only way out of it is to let go of craving. One can't wriggle out of craving. One really has to let go of it. So wriggling around isn't going to get us out of pain or dissatisfaction.

The comfort we lack in the sitting position gives us a wonderful opportunity to learn about our sensual desires. If we don't learn about them here, there is no other place we're going to learn about them. Nobody teaches these things, not in schools or universities. They're not taught in the home. There everybody's trying to be as comfortable as possible. Here we have a ready-made possibility of learning something about our craving, the cause of all grief. If you are sitting comfortably there's nothing wrong. It's wonderful. But if you aren't it's just as wonderful. You have a learning situation right here in your own legs or back or wherever it may be.

The desire for comfort and the wriggling around trying to get it, is exactly what everybody is doing everywhere. People pay a lot of money for it. That's why people work overtime, go on journeys, search for entertainment, to wriggle out of discomfort. But it's a lost cause. Why identify yourself with a lost cause? Once you've wriggled out of one uncomfortable situation, isn't there another one arising within a short time? When one entertainment is finished, boredom may arise again. The right leg no longer hurts because you've moved it. Well, the left leg's bound to start. It's a lost cause. It's foolishness to identify oneself with a lost cause. It's much better to identify oneself with the Dhamma. The Dhamma has been proved to be right. Lord Buddha proved it and all those who have become enlightened after him proved it. It's much better to identify oneself with that.

When your stomach growls in the afternoon and the mind thinks, 'I wonder if it's really necessary not to eat in the afternoon?' or the mind goes back to your own kitchen thinking of all the things you could be fixing there, that's sensual desire. If the mind objects strenuously, then sensual desire's got the better of you. But if you can look at the desire and smile at it and say, 'This is Māra in action' then you've seen Dhamma. It's no use listening or reading stories about Māra. You have to know him as he operates and he has no other place of operation except in everyone of us. He's very happy there, having a marvellous time because we're always giving in to him.

One of the things that the Buddha advocated as an antidote to sensual desire is moderation in eating. And this is one of the reasons for accepting that precept of not eating after twelve noon. Moderation in eating doesn't mean eating nothing. It's eating enough to keep the body healthy. But this is a sensual desire which is easily gratified and one which arises again and again. For some people four, five, six times a day! If we are able to put a fence up against one of our desires, we are going to be able to put up a fence against some more. One fence can keep out many desires. So the one that's so easily gratified and arises so often is the one to start with, and that's what we're doing here: moderation in eating.

Another antidote that the Buddha advocated is not seeing the whole but only seeing its parts. Most of you will know or have heard about the thirty-two parts of the body, which are often recited:

> In this very body, from the soles of the feet up, from the crown of the head down, surrounded by skin, full of these various mean impurities; there are in this body: hair of the head, hair of the body, nails, teeth, skin, flesh, sinews, bones, bone-marrow, kidneys, heart, liver, membranes, spleen, lungs, large gut, small gut, gorge, dung, bile, phlegm, pus, blood, sweat, fat, tears, skin-grease, spittle, snot, oil of the joints, urine.

If you have strong desire for a person, instead of seeing the whole beautiful form of that person, remember that this human being is made up of many small parts instead of becoming entranced with the outer shape, form, and colour, which is only the gift-wrapping. Thirty-two parts of the body start out with 'hair of the head, hair of the body, nails, teeth and skin.' So instead of watching the beautiful form, maybe just see the teeth?

There is a story about a monk, who was obviously an Arahant, in the Buddha's time. A man and his wife had had a very bad quarrel and the wife no longer wanted to remain with her husband. She dressed herself up in all her finery, her best clothes and all her jewellery, because she wanted to take all that with her, then she ran away. The husband took off after her but couldn't find her. She had a head start on him. As the man was running along the street, searching for his wife, he met the monk. He went up to him and asked whether he had seen a good-looking, dark-haired woman in a red sari with lots of jewellery, earrings and golden necklaces, who had come along the road in a hurry. The monk replied, 'I haven't seen her, but I saw a set of teeth going by.'

For us that would be rather difficult, but it illustrates what the Buddha meant: Don't see the whole, because people don't usually fall in love with a set of teeth. They don't get passionate about a set of teeth. When, for example, desire arises to have a beautiful new car which is enormously expensive, if one only sees the outer shape, form and colour, one may be tempted to get this wonderful new car and be in debt for the next twenty years. But if one realizes that this car is made up of a steering wheel, accelerator, air filter, motor, which has many screws and bolts in it, one might not be quite that passionately involved, neither with the car that only functions because its bits and pieces function, nor with the person that only functions because its parts function.

A meditation practice for someone who has a great deal of problems with passionate desire is to look at those parts in themselves. We're all made up out of the same thirty-two parts of the body. Nobody's any different. If we take the skin apart, we find the same thing in everyone.

The one antidote which is the same for all five hindrances – our five enemies – is noble friends and noble conversation. To have the kind of friends with whom one discusses not gossip, not the weather, not politics, not other people, but the way of emancipation through Dhamma. Those kind of friends are the important people in one's life. When Ānanda, the Buddha's cousin and attendant, once said to the Buddha, 'Sir, a good friend is half of the holy life,' the Buddha said, 'Do not say so, Ānanda. A good friend is the whole of the holy life.' There is nothing to take the place of a spiritual friend. This is the most important person in one's life – the kind of friend who helps one remember to be on the path.

It is a matter of remembering. When we remember, we can do it, but most of the time we forget. The noble conversation we can have with such a person helps one again and again to look at oneself and see that our problems come from craving, from wanting.

We don't eat any poison. We don't want to fill our bodies with rubbish food. By the same token, we should not fill our minds with rubbish talk or even poisonous talk. The mind should always be filled with Dhamma talk, righteous talk, the talk that uplifts, the talk that helps, the talk that soothes, calms and heals, that most of all helps us to see our way out of the problems that beset every human being.

When we have the good fortune to have a noble friend with whom we can have noble conversation then it is also our way of repaying that gift by being a noble friend to others. Noble friends are like a chain reaction. We don't only need to search for one. We can also be one.

ILL-WILL

We are constantly tempted to fall into the error of being involved with our enemies. Because they are inside us, it's difficult for us to know them. We must, first of all, try to bypass them and then keep on purifying ourselves so that they will eventually no longer be part of our nature.

The spiritual path, the path of purification, of emancipation, of liberation, is a path where we change our inner nature. Unless we start doing that, we haven't entered the path. Everything else is external. Only that is internal. While externals can be pleasant, can give a feeling of satisfaction, they will not change our inner nature. It is that change alone that makes the difference between a worldling and a noble one. A worldling follows his or her inner nature, just the way it is. A noble one has changed it.

The second of those hindrances, those defilements that create so much havoc within us and thereby also around us, is ill-will or anger. It may be slight. It may be heavy. It may be actually pronounced or just sitting inside. When it is verbalized there is a chance the other person will also get angry. Then we have family disagreements or arguments with the neighbours. We have strife between communities and in the end we have war between countries or in the whole world.

The whole thing starts in our own heart, therefore it is essential that we realize the world is not other people. Each one of us is the world and unless we find peace within ourselves, we won't find it anywhere. It makes no difference whether somebody else is angry, upset, wrong or egotistical. It doesn't matter at all. The only thing that matters is what we ourselves are doing about it. There is never going to be total peace in the world. In the Buddha's time there wasn't total peace. In none of the great spiritual masters' time was there total peace. On the contrary, history tells us about political manipulations and warfare, brother fighting against brother.

The only peace that we can experience is the one in our

own heart. The peacefulness that the Buddha found for himself had enormous repercussions in the world though. He was one man who made peace with himself and with the world, and that peace is still available to us today, two and a half thousand years later, in his words and instructions. Five hundred million people in the world call themselves Buddhists today.

Obviously our kamma is not exactly the same. But it would be quite sufficient if the peace we found in our own heart could extend to our own family. Even that would be a great achievement, don't you think? That would be enough. If it extended to our whole family, every member of it, then maybe it would extend to their neighbours also. An even greater achievement. We don't have to become a Buddha in order to have some wholesome influence over others.

But wholesome influence can only be exerted when there is peace in our own heart, when anger no longer arises. The very tendency to irritation only disappears in Arahants. But having slight irritation in one's heart is a far cry from getting angry or having arguments, being resentful, rejecting others, feeling hurt and thereby justifying resentment.

Anger arises because one feels hurt in some manner or form. Pain has arisen and the absurd human reaction, the natural instinctive one, is to inflict pain too. Unless we become aware of that, we can't change it. Not everybody starts to inflict pain on others, some inflict pain on themselves. They swallow their anger and suppress it and it seethes inside. All that resentment, worry and anger shows itself in physical ailments, lack of energy, depression, negative reactions, a lack of enjoyment and happiness.

Very few people walking along the streets have a happy expression on their face. Have you noticed? You don't have to be here to notice that. You can be in Sydney, in London, in Amsterdam or Paris. It doesn't matter where, it's the same wherever you go. Very few people have a happy expression on their face and equally few have a serene expression.

The hurts that we have experienced in life, with our constant reactions to them, give us the idea that we can eliminate the pain if we reciprocate. On the contrary, this creates double pain. It is another one of those absurd human follies, just the same as thinking about the past and the future instead of living in this moment.

The Buddha compared anger to a bilious disease. Exactly the same words for anger are used in the German language: 'Mir kommt die Galle hoch' – 'The bile comes up.' If you ever had that happen to you because of illness, you know what it tastes like. If you've ever been angry – and I doubt if anyone is spared that – you also know what it feels like. If feels awful – yet people get angry over and over again. If that's not absurd, what is? It's like hitting oneself again and again, every time feeling hurt but still continuing.

The Buddha also compared anger with picking up hot coals with one's bare hands and trying to throw them at the person with whom one is angry. Who gets burned first? The one who is angry of course.

He compared anger to a pond in which the water is turbulent. If you have boiling water, you can't have a clear and calm surface in which to see your likeness. When one is angry it's impossible to know whether there is any purpose being served, mindfulness is lost. One has forgotten all that, one is just angry. If anyone ever had time to look in a mirror when they were angry, they'd be surprised at the kind of face they would see. But nobody has time for that when they are angry. One is engulfed in the emotion.

The Buddha said one of the first things to remember when anger arises is that, 'I am the owner of my kamma.' Such recollections are extremely important to have at your command, to remember them at a moment when it's critical. 'I'm the owner of my kamma, so when I'm getting angry, obviously I'm going to get the result of that.' Whether the other person has done anything to justify your anger has nothing to do with it.

There is the beautiful story of Khantivādin, the teacher of patience. Beautiful, because it exemplifies so well the non-justifiability of anger. The king of Kausala was a very rich king. The story also says that he had five hundred wives. (We must remember that five hundred, one thousand, fifteen hundred in Pali always means 'many.' So whether he had this exact number of wives, or some approximate number, we don't know.) One day the king decided he wanted to go on a picnic and he let the wives know this. The cooks were alerted to prepare the food, the servants to get the elephants ready with seats and decorations and the soldiers to get ready in their best uniforms.

The next morning the whole palace, the royal servants and the royal wives, set out. They came to the forest and found a beautiful meadow for their picnic. The king ate and drank too much. Immediately after lunch he fell asleep and the wives said to each other, 'Now's our chance. We don't often get out of the palace. Let's look around.' They all trooped off and looked at the butterflies, the greenery and the trees and enjoyed the beauty of the forest.

Very soon they came to a little bark hut in front of which sat a very famous old sage whom they recognized as Khantivādin (*khanti* – patience, *vādin* – teacher; teacher of patience). All the women sat down in front of him, paid their respects and asked him to preach a sermon to them. He very willingly obliged and spoke about moral conduct, loving-kindness and generosity.

Meanwhile the king woke up and there wasn't a single wife to be seen anywhere. He was furious. He called the soldiers and said, 'Go! Get my wives back immediately.' They obediently ran off into the forest and found the wives sitting in front of Khantivādin's hut. They went back to the king and reported, 'Your Majesty, they are sitting in front of Khantivādin's hut listening to a sermon.' But the king was still under the influence of all that food and drink and couldn't listen to reason. He told the soldiers to chase all the wives back to the meadow and then tie Khantivādin to the nearest tree. Since they were in the employ of the king, they could not do otherwise. They chased all the wives back to the meadow and tied up Khantivādin.

Then the king took a huge knife, ran up to Khantivādin in great rage and said, 'You old scoundrel, you. You've been trying to take my wives away from me.' And he cut off one foot and said, 'And where is your patience now?' Khantivādin replied, 'Not in my foot, your Majesty.' Then the king proceeded to cut the old sage to pieces while repeating the same question and each time getting the same answer, which increased his fury.

When Khantivādin was on the point of dying, the soldiers who had witnessed the spectacle, said to Khantivādin, 'Sir, please do not curse the whole kingdom. Just curse the king.' And Khantivādin said, 'I do not curse anyone. May the king live long and happily.' And then he died. The story says that the earth then swallowed up the king.

The next day the Buddha was informed of this happening, whereupon he said, 'Who does not act in this way has not understood my teaching.'

The beauty of the story lies in the fact that we have a guideline. We have an ideal. Even if we were cut up limb from limb, there is no reason to get angry. That goes a bit far for us, doesn't it? Obviously Khantivādin was an Arahant because his remark 'My patience is not in my foot' means that although he was experiencing excruciating physical pain, his mind was not affected, and that is only possible for an Arahant. In our case it's not possible. Our mind is much affected by our physical discomforts. But whatever happens to us, it is probably not going to be quite as bad as being cut up limb from limb, piece by piece. If we could remember this story and remember what the Buddha said, 'Who does not act in this way has not understood my teaching,' maybe we could see that the anger which we experience at anything or anyone is only a reaction of our own defilements. It has absolutely nothing to do with the deed or the doer itself.

When we get an idea of that, we have a chance to change, but only if there is mindfulness and we become aware when anger arises. Mindfulness will act like the brakes on a car. If you have no brakes on a car, it's obviously going to be very dangerous. Without mindfulness life is very dangerous.

When you step on the brake of mindfulness when anger arises, you become aware that there is a defilement. There is something unprofitable, unwholesome to work with. With this awareness, you already take away most of the anger's strength, just like putting on the brakes on a car, you can take away most of the speed, and slow down. Understanding this as a defilement already slows the whole process down and can actually bring it to a standstill. As anger comes to a standstill you can take a look at it and see its uselessness. You see the hurtfulness to yourself and the foolishness of making yourself unhappy.

The greatest foolishness that people perpetrate is to make themselves unhappy because of their own reactions. A strong resolution is needed one day – maybe today, maybe next year, maybe next lifetime – to stop making ourselves unhappy. No longer to react negatively to whatever happens around us, because we realize that everybody is beset by defilements and that whatever we experience which is not pleasing to us is due to a defilement.

The whole world is full of defilements. Just look at the newspapers, the international magazines like *Newsweek*. What do you see? Nothing but defilements. If we accept the fact that the whole world is beset by them and made unhappy by them, why not take a step in the right direction and try to stop oneself from joining in this unwholesome chorus? Why not step aside from it and watch it from the sidelines? One can do that when one no longer gets involved with negative reactions of which anger and hatred are the strongest.

People will never stop saying or doing the wrong things. Only when we train ourselves in Dhamma will we have a chance to stop. But we can't help ourselves. If we are confronted by wrong things, wrong reactions, wrong deeds, selfishness, wanting more than we are willing to give, what does it matter? The only thing that matters is the peace and happiness in our own heart. Everything else becomes a totally unnecessary problem that people usually live with. All problems are created by our own reactions and we have the natural tendency – another of our absurdities – to blame the trigger. We get angry so we blame the person that has triggered the anger. We get sad so we blame the person that has triggered the sadness, or we may blame the event. But we forget that it's impossible for us to get angry or sad unless we already have that tendency inside us waiting to be triggered. It could never happen otherwise.

The simile I like to use is the jack-in-the-box, a toy for children, a little box that has a doll inside sitting on a spring. The idea is for the child to touch the lid ever so faintly and then the little jack jumps out. If we take the doll out of the box the child can hit the box with a hammer and still no jack-in-the-box will jump out. There is nothing inside. It doesn't matter what the trigger is. Only what's in there can come out.

The only way we can find peace in our own hearts, find the pathway that leads to liberation, is to change ourselves, not by changing the world. There's nothing to change out there. Everybody has to change themselves. The Buddha did not deliberately change people. He told them how to do it for themselves. It's strictly a do-it-yourself job. Nobody can do it for you and the sooner one starts, the sooner one has a chance of finding happiness, totally independent of what goes on externally.

Very few people in this world have perfect situations. Everybody has something wrong in their lives. Either the house is too small or the salary too low, or the relatives don't agree, or the street is too noisy, or the food is not good enough, or the education wasn't sufficient for the job one wants. There is always something wrong. Nobody has a perfect situation. Everybody tries to make it as nice for themselves as possible, which is all right. But if we do not take a stand now, but keep waiting for perfect situations, we will never change. We can't wait for perfect situations because they'll never happen. The perfect situation can only be created inside one's own heart and mind. There it is possible.

The Buddha said the human realm is the most perfect one for liberation. We have enough suffering, enough discomfort to spur us on to do something, and we have enough pleasure not to become totally depressed by our suffering so we are still in a hopeful state of mind. The only thing that we're doing wrong is we're always hoping for the wrong things. We are always hoping that the situation is going to change; that whoever we love is going to love us too; that the people who are dear to us are going to remain with us or we're hoping that we're going to be rich – if that's what we're looking for. Maybe we're hoping to be so intelligent and wise that we will never make a mistake. Always hoping for the wrong things.

This hope in our heart can be put to great advantage. It comes about because we know there's something wrong and we're not totally depressed by it. We all know there's something wrong. But the only things wrong are the defilements.

That's all. Nothing else is wrong. What we need to hope for is that we shall be able to do something about them right here and now and not in the future, because the future is imagination. Who knows what might happen tomorrow? Nobody does. But we do know right now when one of the defilements arises. We do know when we get angry. That can be known and only that which can be known can be worked with. That which can be utterly and completely known – that is our working ground.

When we get angry about anything at all, the first step is to remember, 'I am the owner of my kamma.' The second step is not to condemn yourself and the third to change the reaction.

The most unpleasant emotion we can experience is our anger towards other people. If we get angry at material objects it is minor, not important and not deeply rooted. Before letting the anger at a person become full blown, where there's no hope of changing it any more, there is a possibility of substituting loving-kindness. People often say quite rightly, 'But I'm so angry, how can I have loving-kindness for that person?'

Some mental acrobatics have to take place. Namely, realizing that anger is useless. It makes one unhappy. It makes others unhappy. Not only that, it also makes a groove in the mind so that anger arises more and more easily. That's why we often find old people are crotchety. Everything around them becomes disagreeable. They're never happy because the negative groove in the mind has become so set they can't get out of it any more.

Knowing these dangers, we look at the person we're angry with and try to remember something nice that person has said or done. That can be effective because if we know the person at all we should be able to remember something pleasant. Everybody does something nice once in a while. Everybody has some goodness in them, so bring that to mind.

If we are already too angry to think anything good of that person, then remember that only an unhappy person acts in a nasty way. A happy person acts and speaks in a happy way and won't make others angry. So obviously that person you are so angry with is experiencing unhappiness. They're suffering. Have some compassion for the other person's suffering whether they have a physical ailment or they're suffering from never having heard Dhamma. One doesn't know what may be the cause. It doesn't matter. Have compassion for that person.

If we're already so angry and can't remember anything good about the person, can't think about their suffering, we can try to feel like a mother towards them. That person's mother surely loves him or her. If we have any understanding of the Buddha's words, as the loving-kindness discourse proclaims, we can remember that person's mother who certainly feels love towards her child and try to arouse a motherly feeling in ourselves.

All these changes in the mind bring results. It will take a while to be successful every time. But by practising continually, it becomes a habit, becomes second nature and when it's second nature one's original nature has changed. Anger, while still arising, no longer has significance or force, because one has learned to change it.

> Who can arisen anger curb,
> Like holding back a chariot:
> Him a true charioteer I call –
> Mere rein-holders are other folk.

Dhammapada, v. 222

Anger need not always be a strong emotion. Anger can be resentment towards other people. It can be the rejection of certain groups of people who don't think or believe or speak as one does oneself. That's very common in the world. It can mean rejecting other people because they happen to have a different skin colour or religion. Rejection of a group of people is the same as hatred.

There may be resentment of one's own lack of material opportunities. Maybe we blame someone for that or resent our lack of opportunity for self-assertion because others get in the way. That too is anger, and it's usually suppressed. One doesn't even admit it to oneself which has major repercussions unless the anger is changed into acceptance and to being at ease with oneself. Suppression creates inner turmoil, which makes it impossible to see anything clearly. One sees everything from the standpoint of that suppression, that resentment.

The Buddha advocated as the antidote for this, loving-kindness meditation and loving-kindness conduct. Meditation as such is all very well, but so often it degenerates into words only and most of you have heard the words so many times. Some people take the words to heart, many people don't. This is the danger of words. This is the danger of externalizing. Often we have the mistaken idea that because we have said the words, because we know the words by heart, because we've chanted them or listened to them being chanted, we've actually done it. All that's happened is that one has created in oneself an inner expanse of devotion to be used for one's working ground. Devotion is love but one hasn't changed oneself yet.

The words are only a landmark, a street sign. They're pointing in a certain direction. The Buddha's words are nothing except pointers in the right direction. They don't do anything for anyone unless one changes one's heart and mind. You know that we can change our hearts and minds. It's even embedded in the language we use. We say innumerable times, 'I've changed my mind. I'm not coming.' We change our minds many times, why not once more?

Loving-kindness conduct is something that we can do deliberately, but it's only a device to help us change our heart and mind. It's not an end in itself. It's a means. The loving-kindness meditation and loving-kindness conduct are both means, devices, tools. They're not the end in themselves. The end is the change of heart.

Loving-kindness conduct – we all know what that means: looking after someone who is sick, inquiring after somebody's health, visiting them in hospital, giving them some food when they're incapacitated and can't look after themselves, being concerned about other people and trying to help them. The further one can reach with that help the better, but one has to start within one's own family as a matter of course. Yet that's only a beginning. Looking after one's own family can just mean looking after the extension of oneself. There are many other opportunities for looking after people. That is loving-kindness conduct. Loving-kindness conduct should not only be confined to a small group, but it should show itself everywhere.

These are the antidotes that the Buddha gave to cure anger, plus noble friends and noble conversation, which give us health-food for the mind.

SLOTH AND TORPOR

I have told you about two of our enemies, but unfortunately we have three more. The first two, of course, you can also call greed and hate, and they are the major unwholesome ingredients of a human being. Not that we don't have non-greed and non-hate also. Non-greed is generosity and non-hate is loving-kindness. It is a matter of cultivating the positive and constantly dropping the negative.

While it's only that, it may sound simple. But it's hard work and unless one is willing to do the work, one cannot follow the Buddha's path. It's the kind of work one has to be willing to do without pause. It has nothing to do with sitting in meditation. This is a full-time job. If we sleep five, six or seven hours a day, that leaves us with something like seventeen hours a day for the work. If we were to confine it to one hour in the morning and one hour in the evening of meditation, it would be impossible for us to make any headway. If we only try to follow the Buddha's way two hours a day and the rest of the time forget about it – this is not as uncommon as it may sound – it's not going to relieve our suffering.

Our third enemy is called sloth and torpor or lethargy and drowsiness, and isn't it an enemy of meditation? I daresay most of you have met him already. It's when the mind is not sleeping, but not awake either. There is a twilight zone, where no fruitful work of any kind is being done. As far as one's meditation practice is concerned it's the same as being asleep because when one is asleep one has no way of concentrating. Nor can one concentrate when one is in the twilight zone. The only difference being that one can get out of the twilight zone a little more easily. It isn't quite as deep as sleep, but it has the unfortunate characteristic of returning over and over again, in and out, in and out.

This kind of mental state in meditation has its equivalent in daily life showing up as a lack of direction which results in lack of energy. It's such a very common experience that a person with energy stands out as an exception. Yet, energy is one of the seven factors of enlightenment. So you can see how essential an ingredient it is for one's mental make-up.

Energy arises when one has a clearcut direction. One knows exactly where one is going and keeps at it. But when the mind has no clear concept of what it's actually trying to accomplish other than staying alive physically, not much energy is produced. It's not fascinating or interesting and the subconscious mind knows already that it's a lost cause. *Nobody* can survive. To use one's strength and direction just for survival is not a fruitful undertaking and real energy will not arise. On the contrary, one feels bogged down and oppressed by it.

The Buddha compared sloth and torpor with being in prison. When one is in prison in a little cell, there's nothing one can do until somebody opens the door. When the mind is beset by lethargy and drowsiness (lethargy is in the body and drowsiness is in the mind) it is imprisoned to the extent that one can only just rouse up enough energy to do the most necessary things.

Most people don't know and don't accept that meditation is a necessity and so the mind easily gives up. One has to be quite clear about the efficacy of meditation. It's not only necessary to eat, sleep, wash and dress. These are automatic survival techniques, and don't need a lot of energy. They are instinctive. But meditation needs energy and that can only be aroused if one knows the importance of it, if the mind is quite clear that this is what one *really must do*.

Sometimes we get so fascinated by a book we can stay up half the night and not get tired at all; we just sit there reading. Or we might go to a party and talk to others practically the whole night and not get tired because we're interested and delighted.

Meditation has to fascinate one. Then there is no reason for the mind not to be alert. At the beginning of the practice, meditation is not delightful at all. It seems bothersome. It seems to be difficult. It has the ingredients of suffering. But when the mind has an understanding of what one is doing, namely watching each moment as it arises, it becomes fascinating to get to know one's own mind. What could be more fascinating? Talking to other people or just reading a book is only knowing about others. But if one watches one's own mind states arising and passing, arising and passing, that is the most fascinating thing one can do *and* the most profitable.

Once Mahā Moggallāna went to the Buddha and told him that he had fallen asleep while meditating. What would the Buddha recommend? The Buddha told him that when he felt drowsiness arising, to open his eyes and look at the light, rub his cheeks, pull his earlobes, move his body to get the blood circulation going and, if necessary, stand up. Anything was better than falling asleep.

These are physical ways of overcoming drowsiness, but there are also ways to help the mind to look in the right direction, such as: life is uncertain, death is certain. Right now is the best opportunity for meditation. There are companions, there is guidance. There is food and shelter, the body is healthy and well enough. None of these things are guaranteed. They are results of excellent kamma. This is a way of arousing the mind energy.

Remember that there is no other moment except this one. The future may seem assured, but that's an illusion. People die every single moment. When we die – which we all will – and are reborn – which we all will be unless we become Arahants – then we have to start all over again. We have to learn to walk, to talk, to eat, to go to the toilet, to dress ourselves. We have to go through the whole school system again, get married, have kids, see them get married. Now you've *done* it all this time. Let's use the time left for what is most important. We've done all the other things. We've already learned to walk and to talk, to dress and to go to the toilet. We've been through school. Many of us have had kids. Perhaps they've got married. Now is the time. There isn't any better time.

If we arouse the energy in our mind for meditation in this way, the energy feeds on itself. It's like having switched on the light. Once it's switched on and the electricity supply is not stopped, the light just keeps on shining.

Meditation does need a lot of energy. It's strange that one should need so much energy when sitting or walking slowly all day. The reason we need so much energy for this is that the mind is constantly trying to do something else, rather than be attentive, so the mind energy is being used up. If the mind were not throwing up all sorts of ideas and hopes and wishes, there would be no tiredness at all. It doesn't come from that bit of physical action which we do here or any other day in our lives. Yet, everybody's dead tired at night. It's the rummaging around in the mind and the constant judging – 'This I like and this I don't like. This one I'll have and this one I'll get rid of' – which is so tiring. That's why people who do jobs involving only mental activity are as tired or more so than people who plant trees or build roads.

When the mind has become concentrated and can stay still, it finally gets a rest. Until that happens we have to arouse it again and again by telling ourselves not to give in. Giving in to our natural inclinations is what everybody else does. That's the instinctive way, giving in to the desire for comfort, giving in to having it as easy as possible. But the Buddha said, 'The one who conquers a thousand times a thousand armies is as nothing compared to one who conquers him or herself.' Conquering oneself means conquering one's natural inclinations and not letting the mind get away with it.

The wish to meditate should have a good reason behind it and only then will we arouse the energy to do it. It's not a good enough reason to want some pleasant experiences. That's not a compelling enough reason for meditating and yet that is foremost in many people's minds. It's very likely to be a disappointment, because the pleasant experience isn't going to materialize very soon. The energy for meditation is lost then because one doesn't get what one wants, and meditation becomes suffering like everything else. An unfortunate mind-trap of wrong thinking.

Meditation has one object only, namely to prepare the mind to get out of all suffering, to prepare it for liberation. It is a means to this end and not for pleasant experiences. Those do happen, and why not? Let us be grateful for them, very grateful that they do happen and that they give us the impetus to continue. But when they don't happen, that doesn't matter either. The mind has to have meditation training in order to become liberated.

The Buddha compared sloth and torpor with a pond where the mud has risen to the surface. If there is mud, of course, one can't see one's likeness. There is no clarity. In that twilight state of half-sleep/half wake there is no real awareness. Even in daily living when the mind says, 'I've had enough. It's too strenuous. I don't want to do it. Let other people do it. Why should I? Nobody else is doing it,' it's a muddy mind because one can't see a clear way, a clear direction for oneself.

A clear direction brings the needed energy. One knows one's path and destination. One can walk towards it with vigour. When one has no destination, there's no fascination, no interest. It's difficult to find a clear destination in life but the Buddha has shown us the way. He has a clear destination of freedom, of cessation of suffering, of liberation, of nibbāna.

RESTLESSNESS AND WORRY

The next enemy is restlessness and worry or distraction. Everybody suffers from that, so you can see what a common enemy it is. All five enemies are unfortunately very common. Everybody has them to some degree. We need to check which one is our own worst enemy, which of the five comes around most often. They are all sitting inside waiting for an opportunity, but one or two of them appear at the slightest provocation and often overrun us. Those are the ones we need to work on.

Restlessness in the mind shows itself in restlessness in the body. The body is the servant, it has no authority of its own. The body without a mind is a corpse. Whatever the body does is being dictated by the mind, whether we are aware of that or not. Most of the time we react so spontaneously and impetuously that we don't even know that the mind has said, 'Do that,' and we think, 'Oh, it's my body,' but it can't be 'my body' without 'my mind.'

Restlessness in the mind is mostly due to past experiences, those one has committed and those one has omitted, all the things in one's life that one would have liked to do and didn't, or those one did and would have liked not to do. Restlessness in the mind makes it very difficult to concentrate because it arises again and again.

The Buddha compared it to a pond where there was a lot

of wind, making the waves rise high. When there are waves in one's emotions, one is drowned by them. One can't see clearly.

Worry is usually about the future and most people are extremely good at worrying and often fail to stop and think how useless and absurd it is. Worrying about the future is meaningless. The person who's worrying is not the person who is going to experience the future. There will be change, not just having grown older and hopefully a bit wiser, but a totally different set of circumstances with different thoughts and different feelings. Quite useless to worry about the future.

If you have some photos of yourself when you were four or eight or twelve or fifteen, hold them up against the mirror. Look into the mirror and decide which one you are. Are you the four-year-old, the eight-year-old, the fifteen-year-old, the twenty-five-year-old, or the one who is looking into the mirror or all of them? If you are all of them, then by now you must be thousands of different people. And that is what one really is, a constant change. If the ten-year-old or the fifteen-year-old had worried about what was going to happen to the sixty-year-old, would that have made any sense? You can't remember what that fifteen-year-old was thinking or worrying about. The same goes for worrying about tomorrow. While we may remember it, although that is unlikely, there's no sense in it. An entirely different person is going to experience it.

That doesn't mean one can't plan. Planning and worrying are not the same thing. Planning turns into worrying when one starts thinking whether the plan is going to materialize. Planning is fine, and then dropping the plan until one can actually put it into action, without being concerned with the future results.

Worry besets most people, and makes the mind tumultuous. It takes one away from the moment, which is the only one in which we can live. Moments spent in worrying are all lost moments. Unless we live in each moment we are missing life. When we think about the past and worry about the future, we aren't living. We are remembering and projecting. That's not living. Life cannot be thought about, it has to be experienced. That's the only way life can ever mean anything, and experiencing can only happen in each moment. This is one of the skills that meditation teaches us, to live in the moment, which means to live at all.

There is never going to be any peace or happiness or quiet in the heart unless we learn to experience the moment. It will remain a struggle to do the things which one thinks one ought to do, to get to the place where one thinks one ought to go, to keep the things one believes are valuable. A constant struggle without ease or joy in it. Peace and happiness are not our birthright. They have to be attained with constant effort and they can be attained if we recognize our enemies and learn to throw them out.

Our inner household is our home where uninvited guests appear. Being hospitable we let them all in. Then we find they have smashed the furniture, stolen the silver and broken the windows. But instead of closing the door and not letting them in again, the next day they are right back. This is our inner household, besieged by enemies. They create havoc inside so that we lack peace and harmony and wonder why. We constantly try to find some external reason and say, 'It's because of that problem I have,' or 'It's because of that relative I have,' or 'It's because of that job I have.' There's a long list of reasons. Everybody has a different list but they all have one thing in common. None of them is real, all are imagined. It's because our internal household is not in order. Our external household can never run smoothly if our internal household doesn't do so. We reflect on the outside exactly what is inside.

Restlessness and worry are not only useless, they are foolish. The Buddha said that we are acting foolishly because we don't see reality. But we have a good chance of changing that, haven't we? Restlessness and worry together are called distraction. We are distracted from what we really want to do, namely to meditate. But it doesn't only happen in meditation, it happens in everyday life also. We forget where we put the car keys. We forget what we were going to do because we're distracted, worrying about something. We don't get our work done easily and smoothly because the mind is somewhere else.

The Buddha explained five different ways of getting rid of

distracting thoughts. He gave very telling similes which help us to remember. The first and most gentle way he compared to a carpenter who has put a block of wood into a hole and finds it doesn't fit. He hammers it out again and puts a more fitting one in. This means substitution. If our mind keeps worrying about the future and remembering the past, it is not fitting. There's no happiness, no peace in that. Substitute! Put something in that fits much better. In meditation, put the meditation subject in. In daily living, put in what is wholesome and profitable. What is actually happening in that moment and has some joy and loving-kindness in it. Substitute!

The next simile he used was of a young man and a young woman dressed up very nicely, ready to go out. They get out to the street and realize that each of them has the carcass of a dead animal hanging around their necks. They quickly run back inside to clean themselves up because they are ashamed to be seen like that. We feel ashamed when our mind is so unruly. We feel ashamed when our mind has all these negativities in it. The Buddha said shame and fear are the guardians of the world. Without them the world would be in an even worse state than it is. Most people think that dirt spots can only be seen on our clothing or on our body. But that's an illusion. The dirt spots on our mind are just as easily seen, not with the physical eye, but with the mental eye. We know when somebody is angry. They don't have to say a word. We know when somebody is egotistical. Their actions and their words betray them. Words and actions come from thought and they must fall in line with what one is thinking. We often don't talk about what somebody has said, but rather what somebody has done because that is an exact indication of what is going on in their mind, good or bad. Remember the dirt spots on our mind are like a dead carcass hanging around our neck. We can take it off and only come outside when we are nice and clean again.

Another simile the Buddha used to describe distracting thoughts was of seeing an acquaintance on the other side of the street. Instead of running over to greet him and inquiring about his health and family and getting involved with him, so stay on one's own side of the street and keep on walking. Pay no attention! When the distracting thought arises don't become involved with it. This is more difficult. To pay no attention means that one is already somewhat in charge of one's mind. It's also a stronger mind action. The first two ways are gentler. To feel ashamed is possible for most people because one has a conscience. But to disregard a thought is more difficult and takes more strength.

The next simile used was of a man running along who realizes he feel most uncomfortable and thinks, 'Well, why am I running. I could be walking.' So he starts walking. He's still uncomfortable so he decides to stand still. He is still uncomfortable so he decides to sit down. Still uncomfortable he decides to lie down and be really at ease.

Recognize the discomfort that comes into the mind and into one's whole being when there are unprofitable, worried, restless, unskilful and distracting thoughts. It brings no satisfaction, no joy, only the opposite. It keeps one anxious and uneasy. Know this discomfort and realize that nobody else in the world can make us comfortable except ourselves. Nobody can do it. Not the Buddha, nor his enlightened disciples, nor the Pali Canon, nor our parents, teachers or friends. We have to do it ourselves. Unless we make our mind comfortable and joyful it will never happen.

These are four methods that we can use in succession, one after the other. If the first one doesn't work, then try the next one and the next one. If none of them has worked then one must use suppression. The simile the Buddha used was that of a great big strong man who grabs a tiny puny man by the neck and drowns him, pushes him under water and keeps him under water by force. In other words, we force those unwholesome thoughts out of the mind and force ourselves not to think of them. This is a last resort, but from it we can see that it's better to suppress than to continue thinking in unwholesome ways. Eventually we can learn to substitute. With the suppression of unwholesome thoughts we do not allow them to make a groove in the mind. We do not allow the mind to become habituated to that kind of thinking. A mind which is constantly thinking either in a restless, worried or negative way, or an angry or self-indulgent way finds it hard to drop the habit. Suppression is better in that case.

One antidote the Buddha prescribed for restlessness and distracted thoughts is learning more about the Dhamma, the teaching. When one knows the teaching, one can direct the mind to it often. One remembers the Buddha's words. When one learns more about it there are clear-cut and decisive answers in any kind of difficulty that arises. The Buddha's answers always lead out of suffering. They always lead out of egoism, but they are not so easy to follow. That's why people often don't wish to follow them because they don't lead to self-indulgence and physical comfort.

The other antidote is to associate with wise and mature people, in addition to having noble friends and noble conversation. This means that one should be careful what friends one chooses. It doesn't mean that one has to give up all one's old friends, but one must find such friends with whom a wise and uplifting conversation is possible. Again we see that the people we associate with are very important. 'Birds of a feather flock together.' The kind of people we're with is a direct indication of what we're interested in.

SCEPTICAL DOUBT

The last of our enemies is sceptical doubt. The Buddha compared it to travelling in the desert without provisions and without a map, thereby going around in circles, being overrun by bandits and killed.

He gave the analogy of a pond covered with weeds. One can hardly see the water at all.

Sceptical doubt is traditionally explained as doubting that the Buddha was really enlightened, that the Dhamma was the truth and that the Sangha had perpetuated the Dhamma correctly. But more damaging for one's personal growth is doubt in one's own abilities, one's own spiritual aptitude.

Self-confidence arises when one is able to do the things one sets out to do. In meditation that means one is actually able to get into deep absorption. Self confidence comes up in the second meditative absorption when one knows that one can do what one wants to do with one's mind. One knows that one has become master of the mind to a certain extent.

Self-confidence has many other facets. It's not aggressive but is a feeling of certainty that we can rely on ourselves completely. That reliance only becomes possible when we have our emotions under control. We cannot be sure of ourselves when our emotions are untamed. When we get upset, angry, worried, fearful, envious, jealous, greedy, when all these things happen in our mind, there is no security to be found. We're not reliable and of course we know that and have no self-confidence. Only when the emotions are brought under control and there is a feeling of rock-bottom security inside oneself that no matter what happens the reaction is going to be mild and equable, then one feels self-assured. One knows one has become a reliable person.

This is an important aspect of doubt because only when we feel confident within ourselves, about ourselves, will we feel confident enough to actually follow the spiritual path to its culmination. Taking one facet of it, trying it out and then trying another one, is much better than doing nothing but isn't the whole path. Self-confidence is essential to be able to say: 'I can really do this, and I will follow it until I come to the very end of it.'

Sceptical doubt arises in people who are unable to love. To commit ourself to one ideal, to commit ourself to one path, to commit ourself to one spiritual activity, we have to be able to give ourselves wholly. If we cannot fully love, we cannot give ourselves fully. Where the spiritual path is concerned, we have to understand it *and* love it. Only then can we give ourselves to it wholeheartedly. If we do not give ourselves to the path with our whole being, it's as if one is married yet constantly thinking there might be some better marriage partner to be found. One can't have a very good marriage that way. We have to commit ourselves totally. Also if we are married and don't understand the other person at all, yet we love them, there isn't going to be a great deal of communication and communion. If we understand the other one, but don't love that person, the marriage is likewise a disaster.

The spiritual path is the strongest commitment there is. There isn't any closer union than that, because it takes the whole person and doesn't even need anyone else for completion. We have to understand the path completely and love it from the bottom of our hearts. When we do that, there's no room for sceptical doubt. One doesn't have to ask, 'Was the Buddha really enlightened?' That's not a pertinent question. If we follow the path we are going to find out for ourselves.

Total commitment means we can give our whole being. If we can do that, it means we are able to love. People who have a great deal of sceptical doubt are always flitting from one thing to the other. In the West we call them 'guru-hoppers.' That's a favourite pastime for so-called spiritual seekers who can't commit themselves. There might be a better one yet. A simile often used is this: You're looking for water on your farm and you think you might find it in the southeast corner. You dig down ten feet and there's no water. Then you think, 'Oh, must be the wrong spot. I'll go to the northwest corner.' Then you go to the northwest corner and start digging. Again after ten feet you give up and think, 'Must be the wrong place.' You do this ten times and never find any water. But if you had stayed in the first place and dug ten times ten feet, you would certainly have found water. Just keep digging in one spot. Commit yourself fully.

To commit ourselves fully to the path of the Buddha is a lifetime occupation. It doesn't mean that we can't keep a house or do many other things, but all of them need to be done with the Dhamma in mind. Then everything we do becomes a teaching and learning situation.

The antidotes the Buddha presented for sceptical doubt are the same ones he used for restlessness and worry: learning more about the Dhamma and associating with wise and mature people.

The Buddha said the one who can get rid of these five hindrances is one who has finished the work, with nothing more to be done. These five hindrances are our passport to saṃsāra (round of rebirth). They are our permanent residence visa. We have to do something about them, if we want to get out. Even a slight improvement makes life much easier. And that's what everyone wants, isn't it? Ease. But the ease we want cannot be obtained through physical comfort. The ease we want can only be acquired through mental comfort and these five enemies represent mental discomfort.

7 *Kamma and Rebirth*

Kamma and rebirth are two fascinating subjects, and are often misunderstood. It's important for us to have a deep awareness of them. We'll have a look at *kamma* first.

KAMMA

'I am the owner of my *kamma*. I inherit my *kamma*. I am born of my *kamma*. I am related to my *kamma*. I live supported by my *kamma*. Whatever *kamma* I create, whether good or evil, that I shall inherit.' The Buddha said we needed to remember this every day. Why is it so important to remember it every day?

The word *kamma*, literally translated, means action. It was used in this way at the time of the Buddha: 'Kamma yoga' means the yoga of action. But the Buddha said, 'Kamma, O monks, I declare, is intention.' It's not just any action, but the intention behind it. Intention is not only in what we do, it is also in what we think and speak. The way we use the word *kamma* is technically not quite correct because we mean our deeds and also the results. However, since *kamma* is in common usage now, we will retain it.

There is a great deal of difference between what we do intentionally and what we do unintentionally. If we accidentally step on an ant and kill it, we probably didn't see it. It may be a lack of mindfulness, but it's not the kamma of killing. There was no such intention behind it. But if we have an ant heap in our garden and wanting to get rid of it we pour poison over it and destroy as many ants as we can, that is the kamma of killing because there is intention behind the act. The

Buddha's genius showed up the difference between 'action' and 'intention.'

What we intend brings results and our actions are caused by thinking about them first. So our thinking is one facet of ourselves which needs to be watched most carefully. This is what we are trying to learn through meditation. Unless we get to know our thinking process, we won't make good kamma, no matter what we do because we won't know the intention. When we know our thoughts, then we can change them and that change will hopefully go in the right direction, in the direction of making good kamma.

Some people think: 'I want to make good kamma, so that I get a pleasant rebirth.' This is a commercial interchange, to do something in order to get something. It's better than not thinking about it at all and just blithely going along with whatever instinct dictates. But it can't have the result one is hoping for, because it's a totally ego-centred approach.

Good actions should be performed because of wisdom, knowing that otherwise there will only be unhappiness for oneself. Goodness is necessary to live in peace and harmony with oneself and others. To consider results is attachment and expectation. All expectations are bound up with disappointments. No expectation can ever materialize in the way one hopes. Expectations lead us into the future rather than keep us in the present. Next life, life after next, or the life after that, which one? What about the next five minutes? Good action ideally becomes so ingrained in oneself that nothing else is possible. As long as something else *is* still possible, wisdom must dictate the right direction.

When two people do the same thing, there won't be the same result. The Buddha compared making bad kamma to putting a teaspoon of salt into a cup of water or putting a teaspoon of salt into the river Ganges. A teaspoon of salt put into a cup of water makes it undrinkable. But a spoonful of salt dropped into the Ganges is going to make no difference at all. If one has a river full of good kamma, one unprofitable, unskilful action will make no difference. If one has only a cupful of good kamma, one unskilful action will sour the whole life. Since we have no definite idea of what we have behind us, we had better presume it's only a cupful. We

sometimes wonder why some persons doing all sorts of unwholesome deeds still seem to live very happily. Family, bank
account, health are all fine. Why isn't he getting his punishment? He's not getting it because he isn't deserving it just
yet. We get exactly what we deserve. It's not accidental, nor
is it chaotic. There's no reason to think that chaos prevails in
the universe. Moon, stars, sun – everything acts according to
a pattern, even this little globe on which we live. It is the
same with our kamma.

Kamma is impartial and this is often forgotten. It doesn't
have preferences. It is cause and effect. It doesn't take indi-
viduals into account. Whatever has been put into the stream
of happening is in there and will eventually bring a result.

We bring certain tendencies with us from past lives, yet
most of the things that happen to us are results of present
actions. We don't have to think, 'Ah, that was because three
lifetimes ago I must have done this or that,' or 'If I do this
now, next lifetime I'll be all right.' This is taking the easy way
out and not taking responsibility. If one takes full responsibility for oneself – and every thinking, intelligent person needs
to do that – then we can also recollect that we have done or
omitted certain actions in this lifetime and that the results are
right here and now.

The connection can easily be found. Whatever skilful, profitable actions we have actually accomplished in this lifetime
show results. They show in our abilities, our strength, our
health, our character. We are the makers of our own destiny.
Nobody else can really do anything for us. If we believe that
somebody else can act for us, we haven't understood what
the saying 'I am the owner of my kamma' means. It's the one
thing we own. Everything else is on loan. We can take nothing
with us except that. Everything else goes to our heirs, those
who come after us. Kamma is ours.

We bring tendencies with us, which create our opportunities. We have choices, but not unlimited ones. We all had
the choice whether to come to this retreat or not. You made
the good kamma of choosing to come. Once you're here, you
have constant choices. When hearing Dhamma, you can either
be half awake and not get much of the meaning or you can
be completely attentive. When listening totally, you again

have choices. You can immediately forget it or you can try to remember it. Should you make the choice of trying to remember it, you then have the choice of actually trying to live by it or remembering it as something interesting. If you make the choice of living by it, you can choose to do so all the time or only on special occasions.

The choice is ours, constantly, every single moment. Every moment except when we are asleep is a kamma-making moment. That's why it's essential to perfect the skill of living in each moment. If we don't watch each kamma-making moment, it's not going to work out on the credit side. There are too many negative moments possible. Each mind moment has to be watched because they are choice moments and these choice moments make kamma. The more profitable and skilful choices we make, the more opportunities we have. It's like living in a house with many windows and doors and having that many choices through which window or door to leave. If we make enough wrong choices, our opportunities diminish to the point of finding ourselves in a prison cell where there are no opportunities at all until we are released. If we've ever wondered why some people appear to have many opportunities to do different, interesting things and we ourselves have not, it's strictly due to the kamma we have made.

The Buddha said that some people are born in the light and go to the light. Some people are born in the light and go to the dark. Some people are born in the dark and go to the light. And some people are born in the dark and go to the dark. This means no matter where we're born, our choices and opportunities exist.

There was a woman called Helen Keller who was born deaf, dumb and blind. She managed to get a university education, write books and be instrumental in helping handicapped people to a better life. Obviously she was born in the dark, but she went to the light.

All of us have opportunities every single moment. If we don't make use of them, the same opportunity may never come again. Because we have lost that one, we have lost one of the windows or doors of the room we live in. Total attention to each moment is necessary.

The Buddha also compared kamma to a spider's web, a

web so intricately woven that one cannot find the beginning or end of the thread. It's impossible for us to know whether we are sick today because of doing something unskilful fifteen years ago, or because we didn't watch what we ate yesterday. The cause and effect of actions and results are so intricately intermeshed that we cannot see clearly how something came about. The major happenings in our life can be seen, however. It's easy to recollect bad choices made because of self-indulgence and the results that accrue from them.

Kamma is really not important as it has come to us from the past or will accrue to us in the future, because the past is like a dream and the future is 'the not yet come.' The only thing of any interest to anyone is *now*. Everything else is like living in a dream world, never being totally awake, never quite knowing what's going on. There's no real joy in that. It has a foggy unreality about it. Everyone who is not enlightened lives in some fog, but one can try to wake up from the dream. Actually there is no moment other than the present one. We cannot possibly relive yesterday or experience tomorrow now. There is only one thing we can do and that's be alive now. But one has to be totally awake and aware to accomplish that. Awake and aware to one's intentions.

Mind is the master. What hasn't been created by thought doesn't exist. It may be created by somebody else's thought, but it doesn't exist for us. Thought is the underlying cause for all our kamma. We have three doors: thought, speech and actions. These are the three with which kamma is made and through which we contact the world.

Although the thought is the basic underlying cause, it still makes the weakest kamma if it doesn't result in speech or action. Let's say we hate somebody and the thought flits through the mind, 'If that fellow comes near me again I'm going to kill him,' but we never say or do anything about it. Although it makes very unprofitable kamma as an unskilful thought, nothing much has resulted, so the kamma is fairly weak. If we think it often enough, then we're putting a groove into the mind which will eventually result in speech. If the same fellow does come near us we may say, 'If you come near me again I'm going to kill you.' That's much stronger kamma. First of all we have created an enemy and we have solidified the thought through speech. If we say it often enough we may eventually come to the deed. Obviously that is the heaviest kamma and will have very strong results. The thought needs to be watched and it needs to be changed when necessary. If an unskilful thought arises one should be careful to refrain from letting it turn into speech or action.

REBIRTH

Rebirth is one of those subjects that often meets with fascination, hope, wishful thinking or total rejection. One of the classic similes for rebirth is the one about the candle. A candle has burned down to its last little bit. A new candle is lit from the old flame and then the old candle goes out and the new one is burning. There is evidently a new body of wax but is it the same flame or a different flame? If you'd have an opinion poll you'd find the answers half for the same flame and half for a different flame. The truth is neither. What you have is a transference of energy. The heat has been transferred. Heat is energy and this is what we have in rebirth – a transference of the heat of our passion for life. Our passionate desire for survival, which does not diminish until enlightenment.

Once the Buddha was asked by the wanderer Vacchagotta, 'Sir, what happens to the Enlightened One after death? Where does he go?' The Buddha said, 'Wanderer, make a fire from the sticks that are lying around here.' So he did and he lit the fire. Then the Buddha said, 'Now throw some more sticks on to it.' He did, and the Buddha asked, 'What's happening?' Vacchagotta answered, 'Oh, the fire's going well.' The Buddha said, 'Now stop throwing sticks on it.' And after a while the fire went out. The Buddha said to him, 'What happened to the fire?' 'The fire's gone out, Sir.' The Buddha said, 'Well, where did it go? Did it go forward? Backward? Right? Left? Up or down?' The wanderer said, 'No it didn't. It just went out.' The Buddha said, 'That's right. That's exactly what happens to the Enlightened One after death.'

There are no more sticks thrown on the fire of passionate desire, of craving, of wanting to be, and the fire goes out. There is no kamma being made by the Enlightened One, so there is nothing to be reborn. With us – in whom there is the craving for survival – that's our passport to rebirth. The heat of the passion is the transference of energy. Sometimes the reverse side of the same passion arises. One doesn't want to live because life is too unpleasant. 'I' want to live or 'I' don't want to live is the same ego-delusion. The desire for survival is our strongest craving. It's so strong that even on one's deathbed, there is very rarely a gentle giving up and giving in.

It is said that the moment of death can be the most favourable moment for enlightenment because one has to give up one's ownership of the body. But most people don't want to let go. Since the body gives up anyway they are forced to do so, but mostly under protest. If one gives up voluntarily, however, that can be a moment of enlightenment. While one is still living comfortably and everything seems to be going rather well – the food's all right, the digestion works, it isn't too hot or too cold, the mosquitoes aren't biting, nobody's saying nasty words – at such times there is no great urgency to let go. Liberation doesn't seem to be the greatest priority then. But at death, it may be the one thing one can still do – namely let go.

What is embedded in the mind through habitual thought, speech and actions creates a kammic aggregate. What is reborn is a genetic blueprint and a kammic blueprint, totally impartial. The Buddha said that it's wrong to think that the one who makes the kamma and the one who reaps the consequences is the same person; likewise that the one who makes the kamma and the one who reaps the consequences is a *different* person. The answer lies in the middle. There is continuity but no entity. There is no individual person who is doing it and reaping the result, but there is continuity. That one isn't the same person being reborn is quite clear because body, thoughts and feelings have changed. Everything has changed from the moment of kamma-making to the moment of kamma-reaping. But that there is continuity between the one who has made the kamma and the one who reaps the kamma is also clear. Kamma runs through our lives. It has our past actions embedded in it, but it doesn't mean that we can say, 'Well, that's just my kamma,' and leave it at that.

There were teachers in the Buddha's time who taught that everything was kamma, which leaves out completely one's own choice. The Buddha denounced this teaching. There were also teachers in the Buddha's time who said that nothing is kamma. It doesn't matter what one does, there is no result. The Buddha denounced that teaching too. There is kamma and there are results, but there is also personal choice.

With reference to rebirth the Buddha compared one's last moments of thought at the time of death to a herd of cows in a barn. When the barn door is opened the strongest will go out first. If there isn't a cow that is the strongest, then the one that is the habitual leader will go out first. If there is no such cow, then the one nearest the door will go out first. Otherwise they are all going to try to get out at once.

What this means is that one's last thoughts create the impetus for one's rebirth. It doesn't mean that past kamma is eliminated, only that our new birth situation is affected. The heaviest, strongest deed we have done will undoubtedly come to mind and give us our new direction. If there is no such deed, then it is our habitual way of thinking that will enter the mind. If we have usually been concerned with love and compassion, that will be in our last thoughts also. If we have no specific thought habits, then what is nearest to death's door will occupy the mind. Hearing is the last sense to go. If we want to help someone who is dying, we could talk to them about their good deeds. What they hear last may result in a favourable rebirth. Without any of these possibilities then the thoughts all go around and anything may happen. One takes pot luck, so to say.

Since we will all experience the moment of death we might as well prepare for it. We need to be ready for this important moment. Preparation for death means acquiring the habit of thinking in a skilful manner. Then we will undoubtedly have a skilful rebirth. It's also said that in order to be reborn a human being we must at least keep the five precepts and not habitually break them. Most people have moments of negligence when some precept may not be observed, but the habitual breaking of one of the five precepts makes a human rebirth very difficult.

There's a story that once the Buddha walked with his monks by the seaside and he said to them, 'Monks, if there were a blind turtle swimming in the oceans of the world and also a wooden yoke, and this blind turtle came up for air once every hundred years, do you think, monks, that this blind turtle could put her head through that wooden yoke?' The monks said, 'No, Sir. That's impossible. They couldn't be in the same place at the same time if they're swimming around in the oceans of the world.' The Buddha said, 'No. It's not impossible. It's improbable, but not impossible.' And he added, 'The same improbability reigns over being reborn a human being.' This should make us reflect that we need to do something useful with the fortunate rebirth we have attained. If it's that improbable, we may not make it again.

Not only do we have a human rebirth – which in itself is a great advantage – but we also have our limbs and senses intact. We have sufficient food and are still healthy enough to sit in meditation. We are also very fortunate to have the Dhamma available to us. One can say that we are on the 'top of the heap,' and if we don't see that as an obligation we haven't understood what it means to be the owner of our kamma. It's not only an opportunity and an advantage, but an obligation as well. We must use this rebirth to full advantage.

There's another aspect to rebirth that needs to be considered: we're all being reborn at every moment. Very few people have the mindfulness or the attentiveness to become aware of that. But we *can* become aware of being reborn every morning. That's not so difficult. The day is over and night falls. Body and mind are 'dead' tired and we fall asleep. In the morning there is a reawakening like a new birth. It becomes light again. Body and mind are fresh and young again and we have the whole day at our disposal to use in the best possible way, just as if it were a whole new life. Look upon each morning as a rebirth and we may understand that only this one day exists. We also may get the idea to use each day to its fullest advantage. That means growth – spiritual, mental, emotional growth. It doesn't mean rushing about and doing as many things as one can.

This is a far more important aspect of rebirth than thinking about one's next life. What will happen next time is completely dependent upon what we are doing now, therefore only 'now' is important. 'Now' is the cause, next life is the result. It's also much more important than trying to figure out what happened in one's former birth. That is all over. That most of us can't remember past lives has a good reason. We experience enough dissatisfaction in this life without having to resurrect the sufferings from earlier lives. A mind still battling with its present defilements is incapable of dealing with such double suffering.

Our rebirth this very morning can bring us that feeling of urgency which is an important ingredient of the spiritual life. Urgency arises when one knows true suffering, the urgency to do it now and not to wait.

8   *The Discourse on Loving-Kindness*

What should be done by one who's skilled in whole-
    someness
To gain the state of peacefulness is this:
One must be able, upright, straight and not proud,
Easy to speak to, mild and well content,
Easily satisfied and not caught up
In too much bustle, and frugal in one's ways,
With senses calmed, intelligent, not bold,
Not being covetous when with other folk,
Abstaining from the ways that wise ones blame,
And this the thought that one should always hold:
'May beings all live happily and safe
And may their hearts rejoice within themselves.
Whatever there may be with breath of life,
Whether they be frail or very strong,
Without exception, be they long or short
Or middle-sized, or be they big or small,
Or thick, or visible, or invisible,
Or whether they dwell far or they dwell near,
Those that are here, those seeking to exist –
May beings all rejoice within themselves.
Let no one bring about another's ruin
And not despise in any way or place,
Let them not wish each other any ill
From provocation or from enmity.'
Just as a mother at the risk of life
Loves and protects her child, her only child,
So one should cultivate this boundless love
To all that live in the whole universe
Extending from a consciousness sublime
Upwards and downwards and across the world

Untroubled, free from hate and enmity,
And while one stands and while one walks and sits
Or one lies down still free from drowsiness
One should be intent on this mindfulness –
This is divine abiding here they say.
But when one lives quite free from any view,
Is virtuous, with perfect insight won,
And greed for sensual desires expelled,
One surely comes no more to any womb.

The Buddha's words
Sutta Nipata

If we stand too close to a mirror, we can't see anything. If we stand too far away we can't see anything either. We need to have just the right distance so that we can discern what we see.

The loving-kindness discourse is close to many of us. We know that it means we should love everybody. That's very true. Especially those people that are troublesome for us and those who don't comply with our wishes or our expectations. Let's take a closer look at the loving-kindness discourse if we're too far away from it, or take a step back from just knowing the words, to see what it really says and means.

It begins with: *What should be done by one who's skilled in wholesomeness...* That is an interesting statement because it explains wholesomeness as a skill, and skills can be learned. We have all learned skills. Talking is a skill. Even walking is a skill. We had to learn them when we were very small and now we do fairly well after all these years. Meditation is a skill and can be learned and is being learned. Driving a car, washing clothes are skills. We learn some of these almost automatically through daily contact in our homes.

Wholesomeness is learned through education and environment, but it's never perfected unless we make a deliberate attempt at it. It doesn't just come to us naturally. We all have some of it, we wouldn't be here if we didn't. The kamma of wholesomeness has brought us here, but we also have the opposite kamma. The Buddha gives exact instructions in the loving-kindness discourse on how to perfect wholesomeness. It's a short discourse starting out with the most mundane, worldly instructions and goes all the way to full Enlightenment. This is called a graduated discourse. The Buddha's discourses are often like that; everyone listening, whether at the very beginning of practice or coming to the end of it, can benefit. Those who can absorb what they hear might be able to use the whole discourse and go from worldly conditions to the supermundane.

The Buddha said his teaching was like the ocean. When we approach it from the shore, it is shallow at first. We can just wet our feet. As we go into it deeper and deeper we are eventually engulfed and finally totally swallowed by it. Just so is the teaching. We start out just wetting our big toe to see what the temperature is. Maybe trying meditation for half a day, then two days, until we finally have the courage to come to a ten day meditation course and sit through all of it. We learn the teaching little by little until eventually our whole life is dominated by it.

The next sentence says *to gain the state of peacefulness is this..* It says clearly that peacefulness is not something given to us. We have to gain it. It's not ours just because we like it or are wishing for it, or because it's desirable. We have to gain it through effort. No gain comes unless effort is made.

The Buddha goes on to say what conditions in oneself are necessary in order to become skilled in wholesomeness and reach the state of peacefulness. These two are foundations for what is uppermost in this discourse, namely how one should approach other people. First one has to do something about oneself. It's no use thinking or saying: 'love, love' but doing nothing about one's own purification.

Then there are fifteen conditions stated by the Buddha which are to be perfected in oneself in order to have love towards the people around one and the world at large. They start out with: *One should be able ...* One should have abilities and not have to depend upon others, but rely on oneself. Self-reliance brings self-confidence, and self-confidence brings a feeling of security. Only when we feel secure can we love. As long as we are dependent upon others, upon their help, assistance and goodwill in order to stay alive and perform the most necessary daily tasks, we are full of fear that those others may leave us. Fear cannot possibly arouse peacefulness. All of us are interdependent, but the fear of being left or of not being able to look after ourselves is an entirely different situation. It can become so fearful that we comply with quite unworthy conditions just in order to keep things running as they are, because we feel so insecure. That's not conducive to peace.

*One should be upright...*A person who is upright not only speaks the truth, which is basic, but also doesn't manipulate people or situations for personal gain. Uprightness is being totally honest, which means expressing ourselves according to our own understanding and not to please others. Uprightness means that we care about truthfulness. The Buddha's teaching is centred in 'the four noble truths.' If we know ourselves to be upright, we are certain not to deviate from the way we feel and understand. We know we are being true to ourselves. Without that, there can be no peace.

The next condition is to be *straight...* which means to be straightforward, not beating around the bush, not whitewashing or flattering. It needs a straight mind. A person who doesn't have a mind that can think straight will have a hard time being straight. It's a skill and needs to be cultivated through mindfulness of mental formations. To know someone to be straightforward makes it easy to relate to that person. We know they mean what they say. We don't have to wonder, 'Do they really mean it? What could they mean by that?' We can trust such a person. To be trustworthy is conducive to having peaceful relationships. If people were to trust each other more and were worthy of that trust, there would be so much less confusion in people's relationships.

And not proud... 'Pride goes before a fall' is an English proverb. To be proud is ego-centred nonsense, be it family status, or possessions, achievements, accomplishments or looks. It's all ego affirmation. But it even goes further than that. Pride creates a feeling of superiority and also stiffens the mind.

There's a story of a Brahmin in the Buddha's time, whose nickname was Pridestiff because he would never prostrate in front of anyone. Not even in front of his own gods, nor in front of any of his teachers. He never came to listen to the Buddha either. But one day he did appear, to everyone's surprise. He listened to the Buddha's discourse, and when the Buddha was finished he went up to him and prostrated. The whole assembly went 'Ahhhh.' Then he made an agreement with the Buddha. He said that after having heard his discourse he wanted to become his disciple, except that he had a reputation to uphold. In future whenever he met the Buddha in the street, would the Buddha accept his lifting his hat instead of prostrating as a proper salutation? The Buddha agreed to that. He kept his nickname Pridestiff until the end of his life.

'Stiff with pride' is the way we express it. The stiffness shows in an inability to accept new ideas and outlooks. Pride is a viewpoint and anything new would endanger the foundation on which the pride rests. It's very difficult for a proud person to learn something new. It's common for such a person to say, 'I know' without knowing.

Easy to speak to... A person who is easy to speak to is one who doesn't resort to anger, rage or fury at the slightest provocation, someone who is interested in what others are saying, and who's able to listen. Listening is an art, which most people haven't developed. To be easy to speak to facilitates good relationships with other people. Others can be sure that one is sympathetic, will listen, will not blame and will try to be helpful.

'Easy to speak to' doesn't mean idle chatter, talking for talking's sake. It means being someone worthwhile to talk to, having developed compassion in one's heart. Without compassion one doesn't become easy to speak to because one is continually thinking about oneself rather than about the other person.

All these skills are needed before there's even any mention of loving anybody. The discourse doesn't get to the word love until all the necessary conditions for it have been made clear.

The Buddha used a simile indicative of various types of people. He compared those who were listening to him to four different kinds of clay pot. The first kind has holes in the bottom. One pours the water in and it runs right out. What is heard is immediately forgotten. The second one has cracks. After the water is poured in, it seeps out. By the time one gets up from one's seat and out of the door, all is forgotten. The third kind is full to the brim. Those are the people who say 'I know.' They either don't listen at all or what they hear makes no impact. One can pour anything in, they are full of their own knowledge and viewpoints. Then there is the clay pot without holes and cracks, totally empty. One can pour clean new water in and it will remain and be refreshing and uplifting to all who drink it.

The next condition is *mild*... Mild is the opposite of aggressive. A mild person has cultivated their heart to the extent where they see the fault in themselves rather than the fault in others. Seeing the fault in oneself has benefit, because one can do something about it. Seeing the fault in others is useless. Usually one just starts disliking the other. Disliking, becoming unfriendly, arguing or trying to convince are all useless. A person who is mild is an introspective person who checks themselves with mindfulness.

Well content... A person who's contented is a person at ease. We need to be contented with our situation, our associates, our income, our looks and our knowledge. It doesn't mean we become complacent. Contentment and complacency are not identical.

Complacency says, 'I'm all right. I'm fine. I've done all I can.' Contentment says, 'The way things are provide the conditions for my growth.' Contentment is essential for peace. Discontent creates all the turmoil in the heart and in the world. Discontent makes us do the most absurd things in order to change what we believe to be the cause. We argue, try to change the people we live with or the country we live in, the food or the ideology, or maybe even the religion. Why all that? Because we are not content. Such actions will never bring contentment. The only way contentment will come about is when we change ourselves. That cannot be done with discontent. It can only be done through patient and persevering effort and a bit of insight thrown in. Without insight, nothing much really happens.

Easily satisfied... To be easily satisfied means that we don't have many personal requirements; not because we suppress them, but because we have seen that they don't make us happy. We don't hanker after new and different clothes, furnishings, food or other material objects. That creates contentment because we are satisfied with whatever we have. We understand that no matter what we buy or get, it's all going to get old and torn and will have to be thrown away in the end, and has nothing to do with contentment in the mind. There are basic requirements to live without great hardship, but we don't need such a proliferation of different shapes, colours and sizes in order to live contentedly.

Desire is painful because it points out a lack. If we are easily satisfied, we let go of desire because we know that we want to let go of pain, of dukkha. If we get what we want we get momentary gratification; if we can't get it, then we get frustrated and the desire is resurrected later. A never-ending vicious circle, not conducive to peacefulness. Before there can be an idea of true lovingness we have to let go of some desires, so that the ego is not always at the centre of all our thinking.

And not caught up in too much bustle... If we have no time to introspect, to inquire into ourselves, we are hardly likely to make any changes. If we are on committees and visit neighbours and relatives, if we create hustle and bustle around ourselves without having some time every day in which to meditate and contemplate, we cannot attain peacefulness. We need time to create a peaceful situation around and inside ourselves.

And frugal in one's ways... Frugality is a virtue. It connotes respect for the work done by someone and respect for their efforts; we don't just throw away their creation at the first sign of deterioration. It also means being satisfied with little, and not trying to always have the best. There's usually something better yet available. There's always a bigger television set, a larger refrigerator, a newer car and a bigger house, not to mention all the other possibilities. There's no end to them. To use our life to attain them is a waste of time, a waste of a good human life.

Frugality means that we can be satisfied with as little as possible, not trying for as much as possible. There is a limit to how little we can get away with, but there's no limit to how much we can desire. Our desires have led us as far as the moon. What else is there to say? Who needs the moon? We can inquire into this and try to make our lifestyle frugal, because that again brings peacefulness.

With senses calmed... The calming of the senses is one of the important injunctions of the Buddha. Our senses are constantly leading us astray. We see something we like and we want it, even if it's only a flower. Seeing something beautiful leads people astray into the absurd activity of plucking and thereby killing flowers, which then can no longer give anyone pleasure.

By being aware we can learn to realise that hearing is just hearing and seeing is just seeing. Hearing is only sound. Seeing is only sight. The mind creates all the ideas around our sense contacts such as: 'This is beautiful and I want it. This is ugly and I don't ever want to see or hear it again.' Our senses are in constant touch with the world. We don't want to be blind and deaf and have no sense of taste or touch or smell. Life would be extremely difficult in such a case, but the senses create a world of illusion for us. They are magicians because upon contact they immediately induce the mind to create the repercussions. It means guarding our sense doors so that, while being aware of sights and sounds and touch and smell, we neither crave nor reject them. This is difficult to do, but a very important aspect of leaving suffering behind.

In the Buddha's time there was a religious teacher of many years' standing called Bahia. Having been a devout and respected teacher for many years, he had got the idea that he was enlightened. For a long time he hadn't had any strong desires or any anger. One night a deva (a god) appeared to him. The deva said, 'Bahia, you're not enlightened. You don't even know the way to enlightenment.' Bahia got quite upset at that and said, 'What? I don't know the way to enlightenment? Well, who does? Quickly, tell me.' The deva replied, 'The Buddha knows the way to enlightenment. Go and see him.'

Bahia inquired where the Buddha was. The deva explained and in the middle of the night, Bahia got up and started walking to find the Buddha. He arrived in the morning, found the house where the Buddha was staying, but the people said, 'We're sorry. You can't ask the Buddha anything right now. He's gone on alms-round.' Bahia said, 'I'll go and find him.' The people said, 'No, no. Don't go. He doesn't answer questions when he's on alms-round.' But Bahia was not to be deterred. He was very anxious to find out how to become enlightened.

He ran after the Buddha and found him in the street walking on alms-round. He prostrated and said, 'Sir, I want to ask you a question.' The Buddha said, 'Bahia, you've come at the wrong time.' Bahia asked again, and again he got the answer, 'You've come at the wrong time.' Then he asked a third time, and the Buddha said, 'All right, Bahia. What do you want to know?' Bahia said, 'I want to know how to become enlightened.' The Buddha replied thus, 'To you Bahia, the seen is only the seen. The heard is only the heard. The cognized is only the cognized.' Bahia thanked him and walked away.

In the afternoon, when the Buddha was walking with the monks, they found Bahia dead on the sidewalk. He had been killed by a runaway calf. The Buddha said, 'Bahia became enlightened before his death.' Bahia had been practising for thirty years and surely in other lives before that and could immediately understand what the Buddha meant with the instructions he gave. When we see something, there is only seeing. But we usually invent a story about the person or object and thereby either desire or dislike arises. The same goes for our other senses, including cognizing, the thinking process. All sense contacts are kammically neutral including the thinking process, unless we start liking, desiring, disliking or rejecting. Bahia understood this.

Now maybe we understand also and can practise. It's possible to do so under any circumstances. When somebody coughs, when the door bangs, dogs bark, when there is movement – these are occasions to practise hearing only sound. When one sees a beautiful flower, just seeing without saying 'I'm going to plant this in my garden,' or, 'let me have it. I'll put it in a vase.' Just seeing and recognizing the thought process which follows the sense contact.

It is said about the Arahants that calming their senses and letting go of desire gives them every power. This is power over oneself, where there's nothing to gain and nothing to lose.

Calming the senses doesn't mean not using the senses, neither does it mean suppressing desire. It means recognizing the senses through insight for what they really are. When there is pain in the leg, for instance, to know it as touch contact. From contact comes feeling, in this case unpleasant feeling. From feeling comes perception: 'This is pain.' From perception comes the mental formation of, 'I don't like it. I've got to move. I've got to get away from this.' Just as we want to escape from unpleasant sights or sounds, here we want to escape from an unpleasant feeling. This practice then means being aware and stopping the habitual reaction. As we calm our senses, our desires will lessen and with that some peacefulness will arise. Desires create restlessness and turmoil in the heart. The stronger the desire, the stronger the turmoil, especially if desire can't be gratified. Not getting what one wants is suffering. Calming the senses leads to peace.

Intelligent... It's interesting that intelligence should be one of the fifteen conditions, because we often think people are either born with intelligence or without it. Obviously that's not so. If anyone lies in bed for three months, they have to learn to walk again. If we don't use our minds, we have to learn to think. Intelligence must and can be cultivated by training the mind through meditation. If we don't meditate it is very difficult to still the mind. The untrained mind goes wherever it wants, from happiness to unhappiness, from worry to fear, from elation to depression, from wanting to rejecting. A mind trained in meditation, can use its inherent capacity to think to the best advantage. It takes intelligence to understand the Buddha's teaching. An intelligent mind is an agile mind that can move, but with direction. It moves where it wants to go and can also expand. It isn't narrowly focused on its old and tried habits, customs and traditions. It's expandable.

Not bold... The Buddha gave an interesting simile about men and women. He said, 'Men are like crows strutting around, looking for their own advantage, and women are like creepers trying to find a tree for support.' Both have to get rid of those qualities. The crow is an example of boldness. At our nunnery the crows steal the cats' food. That's bold, isn't it? They go right into the hallway and take the food from under the cats' noses. Boldness is an exhibition of assertiveness. Self-confidence isn't the same as assertiveness. Self-confidence rests within one's own contentment resulting in feeling secure. Then there's no need for aggressiveness. Nobody likes a person who is bold, asserts himself to the detriment of others like the crow does. But a self-confident person can stand on their own feet without fear, sure of their abilities and potential. There is no need to make others aware of these facts. That wouldn't bolster one's self-confidence, only one's ego.

Unswayed by the emotions of the crowd... If someone gets angry, we don't get angry with them. If someone gets sad, we don't get sad with them. If someone has a poor opinion of another person, we don't agree because it is interesting to talk about such things. We have our emotions under control.

When we don't have our feelings of fear under control, we can experience panic. When we don't have our feelings of hate under control, we get riots. When we don't have our own emotions under control we are swayed by others – gossip, slander, panic, riots, war. To be unswayed by the emotions of the crowd we must be in touch with our own feelings and trust them. We know when they are wholesome or unwholesome.

Abstaining from the ways that wise ones blame... That's the fifteenth condition and means not breaking the five precepts:

1   I undertake the way of training to refrain from killing living creatures.
2   I undertake the way of training to refrain from taking what is not given.
3   I undertake the way of training to refrain from wrong conduct as to sex.
4   I undertake the way of training to refrain from false speech.
5   I undertake the way of training to refrain from alcohol and intoxicants.

Anybody who has any sense would find breaking any of these precepts blameworthy. Getting angry and furious is also worthy of blame, and it's interesting to note how much people want to get rid of that. Not only because it's a fault, but because it feels terrible. Greed and desire are hardly ever criticized yet both are equally destructive of spiritual growth. Both are mentioned here as part of the preparatory work towards feeling some real loving-kindness towards others.

We don't have to go anywhere to ask anyone's opinion. We each have a conscience, which tells us quite clearly what is blameworthy. But we also rationalize, 'Yes, but I had to do it because ...' and then we have a list of becauses: 'because she's so awful, because he doesn't let me, because they always say.' We should stop at knowing, 'This is worthy of blame.' To know a thought, speech or action to be unwholesome is enough. Just knowing, because that will deter us from repeating the same act over and over again. We don't have to be upset at ourselves, saying, 'I'm awful. What is this terrible thing I'm thinking, saying or doing?' That's not loving-kindness. We ourselves are also included in loving-kindness.

There is no rationalization, no justification. Our behaviour skills are just not perfected yet, and this gives us something to do: cultivating this skill. These are the fifteen conditions that are preliminary factors in cultivating feeling for others. Only in the next stanzas does the Buddha talk about loving other beings.

The discourse continues with: *And this the thought that one should always hold: may beings all live happily and safe and may their hearts rejoice within themselves....* If we were to hold this thought 'always,' we would never have any negative thoughts for anyone.

Then the discourse goes on to list various kinds of beings:

> Whatever there may be with breath of life,
> whether they be frail or very strong,
> without exception, be they long or short
> or middle-sized, or be they big or small,
> or thick, or visible, or invisible,
> or whether they dwell far or they dwell near,
> those that are here, those seeking to exist ...

Our loving thoughts should go to all beings, whether alive or seeking rebirth, human or animal, whatever size or form, seen or unseen, in any realm, excluding none. We can only see animals and people, but that doesn't mean they are the only beings in existence. Just because our eyesight does not allow us to see anything else doesn't mean there is nothing more. Bees, for instance, can see ultraviolet light, yet we cannot. Dogs can hear sounds so high-pitched that we can't discern them. What may be invisible or inaudible to us, still exists.

May beings all rejoice within themselves... We think that all beings should live in harmony and happiness. We learn never to harm any of them which means that we have consideration for others. Harmlessness lies with our intentions. *May beings all live happily and safe and may their hearts rejoice within themselves.* If we remember to think in this way, there will be peace and security within ourselves and within those we meet.

The next line says: *Let no one bring about another's ruin and not despise in any way or place...* Let no one do anything to hurt another being. Even if an action is despicable, that doesn't mean we despise the person. The action may not have been wholesome but there is the person's ignorance to be taken into account. If we despise the person, we make bad kamma. It's enough that the other person is already doing that.

Just as a mother at the risk of life loves and protects her child, her only child, so one should cultivate this boundless love to all that live in the whole universe... If we could imagine being everybody's mother – and we may very well have been in past lives – then we might get the right slant on how to approach other people, everybody, bar none. These are the Buddha's injunctions, and he mentioned them as a direction, as a guideline. Once he also mentioned that if we were to lay the bones of all the fathers and mothers we have had in our lives end to end, they would circle this globe innumerable times. If we've had that many fathers and mothers, we must have had that many children also. If we can think in terms of universality rather than of one's own two children at home, then we can expand to the extent where our lovingness reaches out to many. If the whole of humanity are our children, surely we are not going to expect them to all conform to our ideas of what they're going to be and how they're going to behave. They're not all 'mine.' When we think of it in those terms a bit of the clinging we have for what we consider 'ours' may be diminished. A mother risks her own life to protect her children, the Buddha said. This is the way we need to feel about everybody.

That sounds impossible to fulfil, but it really is a guideline to show us what is lacking in our love for others. This becomes very evident when we compare our feelings for our own children with the feelings we have for the neighbour's children down the street. What to say about all beings in the whole universe? It's not impossible to imagine that one could develop concern, solicitude, lovingness, care for all beings, especially if one can see their suffering situation.

The Buddha would sit every morning in meditation and it is said that he then cast his net of compassion. With his divine eye (clairvoyance) he would catch someone in it who could benefit from his teaching. He would then go to that person and teach them Dhamma. He did this for forty-five years, walking long distances to reach people. Such compassion is the compassion of an Enlightened One. We can develop this feeling of motherliness towards others when we see their difficulties, just as the Buddha saw them when he threw out his net of compassion.

Extending from a consciousness sublime, upwards and downwards and across the world... Lovingness to all beings extends from a sublime consciousness, from a consciousness which is not imbued with human problems. It's a consciousness elevated through meditation which brings about a change of awareness. The ordinary consciousness always has some problem that it's chewing on like a rat gnawing on wood. When it becomes imbued with loving-kindness and compassion it has these two states as its focus and lets go of mundane considerations. This kind of consciousness is untroubled.

Untroubled, free from hate and enmity... That doesn't mean that the mundane problems have disappeared. They never disappear. If you think back for a moment, can you remember any day in the last twenty years when there wasn't something that needed attending to? An untroubled mind can be free of hate and enmity because an untroubled mind is a happy mind, and a happy mind doesn't hate.

> And while one stands and while one walks and sits
> or one lies down still free from drowsiness
> one should be intent on this mindfulness –
> this is divine abiding here they say ...

Whatever position one's in, standing, sitting, walking or lying down, not falling asleep yet, one cultivates loving-kindness. Mindful of lovingness like a mother towards all beings. It's limiting for heart and mind to only love one or two or three or even four or five persons, when there are four billion people to be loved.

When one is a mother or a father we should not find it too difficult to gauge our feelings towards others because we know what we feel toward our own children. We can also remember how our own mother acted. With these personal experiences as a foundation we can try to extend our love further.

This is divine abiding here they say... Divine life right here on earth. This creates a feeling of total contentment, security and peace and all other wholesome states accompany it. It creates a mind which is quickly concentrated, which is one of the eleven benefits of loving-kindness. It's a divine way of living now. We don't have to wait until we reach the deva realms.

> But when one lives quite free from any view,
> is virtuous, with perfect insight won,
> and greed for sensual desires expelled,
> one surely comes no more to any womb.

This is a description of an Arahant. *But when one lives quite free from any view...* Any view! The only right views are the four Noble Truths, which include enlightenment. Viewpoints are always viewpoints, not based on valid experiences.

Nazarudin, a great Sufi sage, once said, 'Don't try to become enlightened. Just discard all your views and opinons.' Getting rid of views doesn't mean that we lose our discrimination of what's wholesome and unwholesome in our own actions. But the many viewpoints that people carry around with them keep them in the prison of their own mind-states. How they and others should speak, act and look, what the self and the world are.

...is virtuous, with perfect insight won... Perfect insight is attained with the perfection of virtue as a foundation.

And greed for sensual desires expelled... All sensual desires having been eliminated, with nothing desired or desirable there is no suffering. This is the doorway to Nibbāna the wishless liberation.

One surely comes no more to any womb. No rebirth! This discourse goes from the mundane states of being able and upright, straight and not proud, to enlightenment in the brevity of a few verses. We first develop the heart with loving-kindness to the point of loving all beings as if we were their mother, enabling us to meditate because loving-kindness is one of the three pillars of meditation. Because of using this mindfulness at all times, which means being in the 'here and now,' we lose our viewpoints about self, others, the world. Established in virtue one gains insight and enlightenment follows. A straightforward pathway, no deviations, argumentations, just the doing of it.

This is the essence of this well-known discourse, renowned by word but not so well known by deed. The Buddha gave exact guidelines as to how to purify the heart, how to arrange our life outwardly and inwardly. It's all there for the taking, but nobody can do it for anyone else. You have to do it for yourself.

Once there was a man who came to see the Buddha and said he would like to ask him a question. He said that he had been listening to the Buddha's discourses for a number of years, and during that time had met many monks and nuns who were disciples of the Buddha. He had come to know quite a few more intimately and had found that some of them had changed greatly. They had become loving and kind, wise and patient, but others hadn't changed at all. There were even some who had become far more impatient than they used to be, less loving, and some were most unkind. Yet he had met all these monks and nuns listening to the same discourses. He wanted to know why such a thing was possible.

The Buddha said to him, 'What's your home town?' And the man said, 'I'm from Rajagaha.' The Buddha said, 'Do you sometimes go back to Rajagaha?' The man replied, 'I often go; I have business and family there.' The Buddha then inquired, 'Do you know the way to Rajagaha?' The man said, 'I know it so well, I can go in the dark. I don't even need to see it, I know it that well.' The Buddha queried, 'And if somebody wanted to know how to get to Rajagaha, could you explain it to them?' The man said, 'If you know anybody who wants to go there, you should send them to me, because I can really give exact explanations how to get there. I've gone the way that many times.' The Buddha said, 'I believe you. But if you were to explain to someone how to get to Rajagaha and then that person were to stay right here in Benares, would it be your fault?' The man said, 'Of course not. I'm only the one who shows the way.' The Buddha replied, 'So am I. I too am only the one who shows the way.'

All you have heard, written down or know already, are only landmarks, signposts pointing in the right direction. But unless we start moving along that route we'll remain armchair travellers. The discourse on loving-kindness needs to be made real. There are no superfluous words in it, each is meaningful and directive.

The Buddha also said, 'If it wasn't possible, O monks, to do only good, I would not ask you to do so. It is possible.' He said it is possible to cultivate a mother's love for all beings in one's heart. It is also possible to become enlightened, otherwise he wouldn't have urged all his disciples to do so. It is surely possible to have only thoughts of harmlessness and compassion. Thoughts are of primary importance. What kind of thoughts to think are revealed in this discourse. Thinking determines whether we create inner turmoil, heaviness, disruption or peace and happiness.

The discourse starts out with what one should do to gain the state of peacefulness. It isn't something we are doing for others. We are doing it for ourselves, and that's the only real motivation. Rightly so, because we are the only ones who can eventually change ourselves. That others will have the benefit of our love is a secondary consideration. The primary consideration is our own purification and this should be our priority. First of all we must establish within ourselves a mind of lovingness and clarity. The two go together because the mind that is loving is a mind that has no turmoil in it. The mind without turmoil is a mind that thinks and speaks clearly.

When we establish in ourselves the intention to purify, we can use this discourse to great advantage by checking up: 'What am I doing? Am I following it?' That is one way of making sure that we haven't strayed from the path. No need to blame oneself. It is quite possible to alter our thoughts. It's not that difficult. The more we meditate, the easier it is. We gain strength in our minds, which makes it possible to change our thoughts at will. The one who becomes master of his or her thoughts is the one who gains insight.

9 *Four Kinds of Happiness*

We have in common one thing that is the driving force behind everything we do – our search for happiness. Everybody looks for happiness but very few people find it. The first and second noble truths of the Buddha's teaching clearly state that worldly happiness is a myth, yet we never give up hope of achieving it. This is good, as we would otherwise be constantly depressed at not having found what could make us unconditionally happy.

THE HAPPINESS OF THE SENSE CONTACTS

The Buddha spoke about four different kinds, or grades, of happiness. The first one arises because of contacts made through the senses. The Buddha compared these to a skinned cow, where flies are sitting on the raw flesh, constantly causing irritation. This is an in-depth understanding of our sense contacts. The Buddha also mentions sensory contacts as the first means of gaining some happiness. Most people remain at that stage. We can't always get the pleasure we are seeking and even when we do get it, it escapes us again and again, so that there is no chance of constant happiness through our senses. There is happiness at those times when the sense contacts are pleasant. There is unhappiness when the sense contacts are unpleasant, when the body is uncomfortable or we don't hear the words we'd like to hear, we don't taste what we like or we smell what is unpleasant or see sights which we'd prefer not to see. Nobody avoids such experiences in life. It's impossible to go through the whole lifetime without unpleasant sense contacts.

It's also impossible to go through a whole lifetime without

pleasant contacts. We have, one might say, a fifty-fifty possibility, if we have good kamma. Half the time our contacts are pleasant and fine and half the time they are not. Most people keep on trying to increase the pleasant contacts and hope to make them happen one hundred per cent of the time, which is impossible. There's no chance of success, yet most people continue to try. Most of us blame external events when unpleasant or painful feelings make us unhappy. The real reason, of course, lies inside us because of our reactions to sense contacts.

The more a person is purified, the more pleasant sense contacts will be. A pure heart and mind will find enjoyment in the simplest things. In a beautiful sky, lovely greenery, a pleasant conversation.

Anyone who has not purified themselves very much might not even notice these things. They might never look at the sky or the greenery. They might search for pleasant contact through much grosser possibilities. Drink or drugs, indulgence in food or sex might seem their only obvious sources of enjoyment.

There is nothing intrinsically wrong with enjoying the pleasures of the senses when they are harmless and refined. The Buddha called them a danger though because we so easily make them our goal and direction; we try to get more and more of them or to keep them, try to make them permanent, not to lose them. That's what goes wrong with us, because it's an untenable proposition. There's no way that we can make it come true. No sense contact can be permanent. In fact it would become very unpleasant if that were the case. There's also no way of making sure that we get pleasant sensations. Trying for them takes up our time and energy and leaves no room in our lives for meaningful pursuits.

Our senses are with us. We can't deny them and there's no reason to do so. But it is possible through mindfulness, to realize that the pleasure we get through them is fool's gold. It glitters but it has no value. The glitter can be enjoyed but one should not attach any importance to it. Yet again and again problems arise for people, because they can't get what they want through the senses.

DEVA HAPPINESS

The next step in happiness is called the deva happiness. But it doesn't mean that we have to become devas, that we have to first die and then get reborn in the deva realm; that sounds like pie in the sky. It doesn't seem to have any bearing on our present lives. The deva happiness is the happiness that comes to a person who has cultivated the four divine abidings, the four emotions of loving-kindness, compassion, joy with others and equanimity. That kind of happiness can be compared to living in heaven upon earth. Such happiness is independent of the five senses and only dependent upon our own minds. The underlying condition is the purification of the heart so that it contains only lovingness and compassion. Both lovingness and compassion are qualities of the heart, just as intelligence is a quality of the mind, and they can be cultivated. When that has been done, happiness is one's own. Other people benefit also, but the primary result is one's own happiness because the heart is totally independent of being influenced by outside occurrences. Whatever people do or say, what happens or doesn't happen in the world has no bearing on oneself. When the quality of the heart has been cultivated and has been made pure and full of love and compassion, nothing can touch it. There's peace, harmony, ease and a feeling of security in heart and mind.

This is a far greater happiness than the pleasure obtained through one of the senses. While in itself it does not lead to or have as its result liberation, it is a necessary ingredient on the path.

Lovingness and compassion alone don't produce insight. They smooth the waves of emotions. When those waves of grief, pain, lamentation, worry, fear and anxiety, envy and jealousy, dislike and resentment have finally come to rest, there is a clear reflection without any obscuring ripples in it, like a mirror, the mirror of the mind. That mirror of the mind makes it possible to get a clear vision. Without cultivating these purifying qualities it's not possible to develop further. It's all very well to understand, to know and to quote, but it doesn't take one to the end of suffering. The waves of emotion are obstructive. They not only get in the way of clear vision, they even obstruct the vision of the path itself. When there are waves, one can no longer see where one is going. Indeed one might even forget that one is going anywhere at all.

The happiness of the deva realm doesn't depend upon rebirth. It's possible right here and now. It's internal work which can be done by anyone at any time. There are no special times such as meditation courses or special people who can do it. This is a happiness which of itself, without going any further, creates a different kind of life for the one who has done the internal work.

THE HAPPINESS OF CONCENTRATION

The third kind of happiness is the happiness of concentration which comes from meditation. That too is only possible if one has achieved purification in moral conduct, generosity and loving-kindness in the heart. It doesn't require perfection because that is reserved for the Arahant. It does require some expansion of heart and mind.

The happiness one gets from concentration is glimpsed often by meditators. But one needs to cultivate such concentration and practise diligently to enter into the meditative absorptions. There are different degrees of meditative absorptions resulting in different degrees of joy, bliss and ecstasy. They all enable the mind to carry some happiness with it even outside meditation.

A person who can enter meditative absorption and experience that kind of happiness is someone who can find happiness even when the sense contacts are unpleasant. Such people know they can return to the happiness of the concentration, the meditative absorptions at any time. Knowing that creates a feeling of ease in the heart because nothing else appears to have great significance. When a person is able to go into the meditative absorptions at will for the length of time they wish, that becomes their reality and not the quarrels and the arguments, the inflation and the wars, the future or the past and all the other things that people worry about. None of that has real significance. The reality lies within the happiness of the meditative absorptions.

The meditative absorptions also prepare the mind. They give the mind not only the ability to be happy, but also the ability to penetrate. The mind that can stand still at will is a mind that has gained strength. The ordinary mind finds it very difficult to stand still. It has a jelly-like quality. It shakes constantly. It doesn't need a trigger – that's its natural mode of behaviour. It doesn't have the strength to penetrate the brick wall of delusion. It's not a very good tool, is it? Jelly disintegrates at the slightest contact. A jelly-like mind disintegrates at the slightest blame, at the slightest worry or fear, at the slightest bodily discomfort. A jelly-like mind goes to pieces. What else can it do?

A mind that can stand still is a mind that has the quality of a rock, solid, unmoving. A rock is a better tool than jelly with which to penetrate a brick wall. A rock-like mind isn't going to disintegrate at the slightest impact. It has the strength of a finely honed tool, with which we can pierce this apparent reality in which we live and reach absolute reality.

There are eight different stages of meditative absorption and they are like eight rooms in a house. If one has finally found the front door with the right key and opens it up and goes into the first room, there is no reason why one can't walk into all the other seven rooms also. It is not so difficult to find the front door and put the key in. The key is called mindfulness of breath and the front door is found when one continues with determination and perseverence to keep on meditating. One doesn't sit back and say, 'That's enough, my knees are hurting,' or 'What's the use?' or 'Maybe next life,' or 'It's too difficult,' or any of the many other excuses.

The Buddha said, 'A fool says: "It's too early. It's too late. It's too hot. It's too cold. I'm too full. I'm too empty."' The front door is there for everyone to find. We have the key. We have to fit it into the lock. When we open the door, we find that the rooms in this house are splendid. The splendour is within our own hearts and minds but at present it's locked up. We have no access unless we create it through meditation. Most people never unlock it because they don't know what the key is nor do they know that there is such an entrance. We are very fortunate to know the door and there may already be a small opening through which the light is shining.

When the concentration has been constant for some time the mind becomes very quiet and so does the body. Every single moment of concentration is a moment of purification. The defilements which beset us, causing our unhappiness and difficulties, are momentarily laid aside. The more often we lay them aside, the less habitual they become. The more often we can concentrate, the more often we are without them. Having a pure, bright mind then becomes our second nature.

Concentration starts out with the experience of pleasant feelings. These pleasant feelings arise because the mind at that stage is untroubled. This indicates clearly that if one were untroubled and had a pure, bright mind at all times, one would constantly have pleasant feelings.

Here we get an indication of what is possible, which makes us want this state more often. This desire for the wholesome and beneficial will eventually bring us to the point of no desire, finally eliminating all dissatisfaction.

Concentration starting out with pleasant feelings goes on to the next stage, where there's happiness. Again this is a clear indication that the pure mind knows only happiness. If there's unhappiness, there's impurity. The two go together. A happy person doesn't gain joy through sensual desires, because they know how elusive such joys are. A truly happy person is someone who is joyfully independent of outer conditions. Such a person can concentrate and thereby find a home for the mind where it can be totally at ease. But also that person has achieved purification to the point where unhappiness no longer arises. Unhappiness is caused by defilements. When unhappiness arises we can investigate its cause and invariably we will find an underlying defilement. If we don't find that, we haven't investigated well enough.

In the concentrated states the mind lets go of the five hindrances. When pleasant feelings and happiness have arisen, peacefulness and equanimity follow. Equanimity results in a feeling of having no desire left. Sometimes people even think that they have become permanently desireless, which is, of course, a misconception. But at least for that moment there's no desire.

That in itself is a very valuable experience in as much as

one gets to know a state of 'no desire.' It's utter bliss, the only bliss worth having. When one experiences it, then one knows what one is striving for. One isn't striving to *get* anything. One is striving to *get rid* of everything. This is an interesting misconception in most people's minds. When one first starts meditating one hopes to get peace, happiness and bliss, some of which may actually arise but only if one has let go of something else. Namely one has to let go of some of our ego-supports and most of our desires.

When the bliss of 'no desire' is experienced momentarily we know that's what we really want. But we have to see clearly that it isn't the bliss as such but the cause for it which needs cultivating. That means renunciation, giving up. Without renunciation, life is a constant striving for something. Renunciation is the answer to all kinds of achievement syndromes, not just in the material world, but even in the spiritual world. Trying to achieve something in the spiritual world is just as foolish as trying to achieve something in the material world. There's nothing to achieve. There's only letting go. As we let go, more and more, of ego identifications, desires and support systems, bliss will arise.

Happiness which arises through concentration is based upon purity. A similar happiness can be experienced in one's daily life if purity has been cultivated. In the meditative practice pleasant feelings, happiness and equanimity become deeper and more profound than in daily living, but unless one has already attained some purity in one's ordinary life, one won't be able to do it in meditation either. Daily living and meditation go hand in hand. The harder it is to get a pleasant feeling in meditation, the more purification one needs to practice. There's no blame attached to any of this. These are just states of development.

Happiness of concentration is often considered to be the ultimate achievement anyone can have. That's a misconception because such happiness too is impermanent and not independent, nor unconditioned. It's conditioned by many factors: that there is a certain amount of quiet around one, that the body is still in a fair condition so that it can sit still, and that one can concentrate. Although this kind of happiness is independent of outer conditions entering through the senses, it's dependent upon the inner condition of mind and body. It cannot be the greatest happiness yet.

THE HAPPINESS OF INSIGHT

The greatest happiness, the fourth stage, is the happiness of insight. This is irreversible. Insight, in Buddhist terminology, is always directed towards impermanence, unsatisfactoriness and non-self, either one of the three or all three. If one sees one of the three characteristics clearly, then one knows all of them because they are totally interconnected.

The happiness and bliss of total insight means that one has shed the burden of ego delusion. When one can let go of that, the relief and release is immense.

Ramana Maharshi, who was a sage in southern India, compared ego delusion to people taking a train journey. They enter the train and stand in the aisle holding on to their luggage instead of putting it in the luggage rack and letting the train carry it. Like this we carry the burden of ego around with us when we need not. Ego delusion makes everything seem to be threatening or attacking us, or occasionally defending us, difficult to master, an obstacle, like a mountain which has to be climbed. It can make life look quite difficult.

Defilements are either wanting or hating, being without energy or being worried, anxious, resisting or defending one's own viewpoint. 'But when one lives quite free from any view, is virtuous with perfect insight won' – that's a description of an Arahant. Our own viewpoints are our downfall. The minute we start defending them we can be sure that we are only defending ego. The defence of a viewpoint is an indication that it is not based on experience. Experience needs no defence. The Buddha's teaching is experiential. Viewpoints are based on ego. None of them are absolute truth.

Insight into the constant flux and flow of all phenomena, including ourselves, brings the understanding that there's nothing in this world worth keeping, worth holding on to. Insight releases one from that resistance to other people's viewpoints which can make life so immensely difficult. Other people have other viewpoints. The only answer to that is:

'May they live long and happily.' Attachment to one's own viewpoint only shows that one hasn't yet grasped impermanence. When one sees constant change in everything, so that one can never really say 'I am this,' then a first breakthrough into depth perception happens. Which one am I? Am I the one sitting here who had a good meditation yesterday, or the one who had a lot of distractions today, or the one who's angry or the one who's resisting, or the one who's accepting and devoted? Which one? If I'm all of those, what a conglomeration of people I am! I must be a whole tribe of people instead of just one. So either I'm none or I'm all of them. We'll have to make a choice. If we don't want to be 'none,' then, of course, we choose to be all of them. Then we have to imagine that there are at least a million different people in oneself. That's not an exaggeration, because by this time in our lives we must have had one million different ideas, feelings, viewpoints, reactions over the years, in this lifetime alone. If we choose to be that many different people, life becomes even more complicated than if we were none of them. How about choosing to be none of them?

This insight is very threatening to our ego concept. Why is that? Because 'I' want to be! To be what? To be whom? To be where? For what reason? All are viewpoints, conditioned through our thinking processes. The happiness which arises when one lets go of all that, is the happiness which is embedded in acceptance and peacefulness. Nothing needs to be achieved, accomplished or changed. All is as it is.

The four stages of happiness which start with sensual desire and lead through into insight are a continual purification process. The only way any of this can be verified is through our own experience. For that our own inner work has to have priority. There are no holidays when doing that work, whether we are at the beach or in the meditation hall, driving a car or flying in an aeroplane. There's no respite. In order to graduate from sensual desire we can put our attention on service to others. That means on love and compassion. Service to others means forgetting self. When one gives service to others, it doesn't matter whether one is helping them to wash their feet or helping them to meditate. There's no difference. Love is service, service is love. Concentration is supported by the lovingness in one's heart. One of the eleven benefits of loving-kindness is that the mind is quickly concentrated.

Concentration must not be considered the goal and the end. It is only the means. It is the means for cultivating a mind which is able to penetrate reality. There are two kinds of reality: relative and absolute. Everyone knows relative reality. There we find woman and man, young and old, poor and rich, stupid and intelligent. There are animals, trees, flowers, stars, moon and heaven, and all are judged whether they make 'me' happy. In absolute reality, there's none of that. There are physical manifestations of mind-made objects. That's all. There isn't a single 'me' nor a single 'you.' Nothing – just manifestations that are constantly changing. Even the universe is constantly changing, contracting and expanding. And so are we.

The mind that has become concentrated, happy and peaceful is a mind that can accept this constantly changing universe and use it for its own benefit. The mind that is not peaceful rejects such reality out of hand and says 'But I want to be happy.' That's the mind of most people in the world. The mind which doesn't need any outer conditions for happiness is the mind that can say, 'This is the release from all suffering. This is true happiness.' Such a mind sees with clarity the absolute reality of what's happening in this universe and doesn't have to hang on to anything, attach to anything, doesn't have to *become* anything, doesn't have to *be* anything. It just does what is necessary at each particular moment and then lets go.

The happiness of insight is not exhilaration or elation. It's the sort of happiness which has peacefulness as its base and a lack of desire, striving and delusion as its result. When delusion is gone, the pure bright mind knows only that which is real.

10 *The Five Aggregates*

...in brief, the five grasped-at groups are suffering
and they are as follows:
the grasped-at group of the body,
the grasped-at group of feeling,
the grasped-at group of perception,
the grasped-at group of mental formations,
the grasped-at group of consciousness,
for full knowledge of which,
while the Exalted One was still alive,
he has frequently instructed disciples in this way –
this section of teaching taught by the Exalted One
amongst disciples was thus –
many times has he emphasized:
body is impermanent,
feeling is impermanent,
perception is impermanent,
mental formations are impermanent,
consciousness is impermanent,
body is not self,
feeling is not self,
perception is not self,
mental formations are not self,
consciousness is not self ....

Compiled from the words of the Buddha

When one begins meditation there's enthusiasm. 'I'm really going to do this now as well as I can.' After a few days, one gets used to it. Then the mind starts thinking, 'Isn't this ever going to end?' I can assure you, it will. You see, everything ends. Nothing lasts forever.

When the mind talks like that, just watch, be aware and say, 'Are you playing games with me again?' Don't believe a word the mind is saying. You don't believe everything it says outside meditation. So why should you believe what it says during meditation? It's as unruly in as out of meditation. It just plays games with us.

Every time the mind makes such statements as, 'I've had enough, I'll never get enlightened' or 'I'm doing so well, I can go home' you can just answer, 'Be quiet. I'm going to meditate.' It's a matter of determination, one of the ten virtues. One can't get along without it.

The mind also has other things to talk about. It wants to entertain itself with all that is lacking for its sensual enjoyment. It's used to having far more sense stimulations, more entertainments. It's used to having discussions, going from one place to another, seeing different sights, going shopping and choosing what it prefers. It's used to meeting different people. Here we see the same old faces again. Nothing new. Nothing to discuss. It's used to getting different kinds of food every day and deciding what it wants to eat. Here it has to take what's there.

All these things are irksome to the mind because it wants its own way. The ego says: 'I want it my way and no other way.' We are so used to believing this, that we don't take time to investigate this attitude. If we did we would soon know: this is desire, craving which creates nothing but suffering. That is all it can ever create.

When the mind starts acting in this way, talk back to it. Be your own mother. Tell the mind that it's behaving like a child and that you are the mother, that you are looking out for its welfare and that you know what's good for it. Be both mother and child. Ordinarily we are fifty or a hundred different people. Thinking good thoughts, thinking nasty thoughts, feeling good about other people, creating havoc inside. We have all sorts of personas. Here we can be mother and child. The childish one wants everything its own way, and the mother says, 'No. We're going to do it the best way, which may not be the easiest, but the most skilful.'

The reason for these difficulties has been explained by the Buddha in the five aggregates of clinging. Which are what we consist of. They are all there is to us. Yet we make something out of them, which isn't there. Again the mind plays games so successfully that everybody believes it.

THE BODY

The five aggregates of clinging have as their largest and most noticeable object, the body. Nobody can forget that and everybody has some sort of problem with it. Not necessarily consistently but now and then. 'I can't sit. My knees are hurting. My back's hurting. My tummy is hurting. I'm feeling dizzy. I'm feeling tired.'

The Buddha said that the unenlightened, untrained disciple has two darts or two arrows that are hurting him and the enlightened, trained disciple has one. The two arrows are mind and body and the one is the body only. The Buddha also fell ill sometimes but he continued to teach. It didn't stop him at all. In the end he became very ill, and when he was on the verge of dying he went into the meditative absorptions and thus passed away. Having very bad stomach cramps was no deterrent to him.

The enlightened, trained disciple also has body problems and difficulties. This body just isn't perfect and never totally satisfactory. The unenlightened, untrained disciple is affected by that, a reaction arises in the mind and responds with: 'I'm feeling badly. I can't do this or that because of my condition; my body hurts so that I can't sit up or lie down or stand,' or whatever it may be that feels uncomfortable. The worst of it is constantly trying to adjust one's activities to the way the body dictates. Is it ever possible to adjust one's situation totally, so that the body feels perfectly all right? Has anyone yet found that situation where the body always feels perfect? You can move from here to there, from one climate to another, from a chair to a couch, from the couch to the floor and back to the chair. What happens? Nothing! There's always a problem. So we might as well stay on this pillow.

This body, which is the first one of the five attributes that we consist of, has as its characteristic a changeable nature. Nobody will deny that. But the changeable nature automatically brings unsatisfactoriness with it. If we find a comfortable position it doesn't stay that way for more than five or ten minutes. Discomfort arises again and again. Even at night, on the best mattress, the body still moves.

Because of the body's inherent nature of change, there is constant friction. The movement of the blood, of the lungs, the heart and the breath – all necessary to staying alive, but each movement creating friction. It's impossible that it doesn't. With that movement comes subtle discomfort. The more awareness one has, the more one knows this discomfort. The more one can also realize that as long as there is a body, there will never be total satisfaction gained through it. Eventually the body and its demands have to be disregarded. It always has new demands. Once it's full of food, it wants to clean out its bowels. Having done that, it wants to get new food. It's always reaching for something, never satisfied. It can't be. Because it is constantly changing, it needs repetitive input and outflow, otherwise it can't even stay alive.

Over and over again the Buddha recommended mindfully putting one's attention on the body as the path to liberation. Whoever does not observe the body with mindfulness has not seen the path to the deathless, he said. This encourages equanimity about the useless demands of the body and also brings more insight into the fact that to say, 'this is my body' is an illusion. If it were 'my body,' if I really were the owner of it, why doesn't the body behave the way I'd like it to behave? Why doesn't it stay young, beautiful and healthy for as long as we want it to? And even when it is young, beautiful and healthy, why does it have demands which we can't satisfy, namely constant comfort? Even then, the sitting position in meditation becomes unpleasant. Why doesn't it listen? Why does it die when we want to live? Why do other people's bodies die when we want them to live?

Either it's total chaos or there is some misconception in our mind about body, self, life and death. There is a strong feeling in each one of us that this body is mine. Yet there's very little one can do with it, except constantly comply with its demands. Put it to bed when it's tired, get it to the dinner table when it's hungry, give it something to drink when it's thirsty, make it move when it's uncomfortable. We adhere to its demands and are not really in charge of it.

Mindfulness, which puts full attention on the movements and the characteristics of the body, can eventually see with clarity that the body is nothing but a conglomeration of parts which happen to be working in some manner and fashion as long as there's life. The parts hardly ever work quite perfectly, otherwise there wouldn't be any aches and pains, and they only keep going for a certain number of years.

We call this body 'mine,' creating the illusion of a 'me.' We think, 'I know what I look like. When I look in the mirror I see "me" and I actually know this is "me".' Yet, were we to make a closer examination we would find thousands of 'me's,' all different sizes, shapes and colours. Sometimes a little fatter, sometimes a little thinner, first short, then taller, having black hair, then grey hair, having no glasses, later with glasses, feeling miserable, then feeling wonderful. The question must arise, 'Which one is me?' If the answer is, 'I'm all these different people,' we have at least seen that we're not one, but maybe a hundred thousand people, as we've already discussed. Which one of the hundred thousand can we pick out to be the real me? There has to be somebody that's real to keep the 'me' going. It's impossible for one person to be a hundred thousand people. It doesn't work, does it?

We may think, 'I'll pick the one I am this moment.' But then what about the next moment? What about ten years from now? Always the one in this moment, that's me. We wind up with a constantly changing 'me' which is sometimes hardly recognizable. Yet we think this is my body and attach great importance to it. Of course we have to look after our bodies. It would be foolishness not to. But to let our bodies dictate our lives is futile, because the body will never be satisfied. Even at one's last moments, the body still craves comfort. There are several meditation techniques the Buddha mentioned in the discourse on the foundations of mindfulness which help one to lose some of one's attachment and ego illusion about the body.

There has to be a balance between calm and insight. Insight is essential and can result in the unconditioned. Calm is always conditioned by the ability to concentrate. If anything happens to the body and the body is no longer able to sit, the calm will be gone because insight has not arisen. Insight about this body has to be part and parcel of the spiritual path.

The meditations that the Buddha advocated in the foundations of mindfulness discourse are called the charnel-ground meditations: nine different ways of seeing one's own dead body. We are definitely going to be dead, so we might as well accept it now and not wait until it happens. We might even now shake with fear everytime the heart misses a beat or we don't feel quite as well as we used to when we were seventeen. One of the ways of meditation on death is seeing oneself as a skeleton. Look at it sitting there in the meditative posture. Next take the skeleton apart and lay the bones out one by one. Then let the bones crumble to dust. It takes away some of the ego illusion and the attachment to this body.

One of our impediments is desire for physical comfort. It doesn't allow us to stay up at night because we could be too tired. It asks us to protect ourselves from mosquitoes and flies, from cold or hot weather, from any potential discomfort. We are busy protecting ourselves and spend much precious time on that.

It's one thing to know that we're going to die, but it's another thing to actually see one's death with one's inner vision and accept it with equanimity. Try it in your next meditation session for a few minutes. See yourself dead and watch the reaction. The first reaction may be, 'I can't do it and I don't want to do it.' Try again. The foundation of mindfulness discourse is so well-known because it provides the way to the deathless state which is liberation. Most people come to a meditation course because they want to get some peace and quiet. They want to get away from it all and find some bliss, joy and happiness which they can't find at home. Fine. But that's only one aspect of the Buddha's teaching. The Buddha called this 'a pleasant abiding' and it relies on favourable conditions. Some people have already experienced the fact that their body is making it impossible for them to meditate. Some of them are lying down and some of them have even gone home, because the mind is reacting to discomfort. We are all prone to this danger. Let's know the danger before it happens and do something about it by seeing the body as it actually is.

FEELING

The next of the five attributes that we consist of is feeling. It plays another very important part in our ego illusion, because we believe feelings to be ours. I'm feeling well or unwell or I'm feeling happy or unhappy. Yet, if they are ours, why don't we have jurisdiction over them? Why can't we constantly feel well, constantly feel happy, alert, at ease? Why not? Who is in charge of all of this?

The ego illusion arises because we believe body and feeling to be ours. Yet when we examine them, we must come to the conclusion that we really have no say in the matter. It's all just happening. How do we come to think it's 'me'? When there's any feeling of discomfort, sadness, boredom or frustration, we become uncomfortable, sad, bored, frustrated. We react by being involved with the feeling instead of knowing that this feeling has arisen and will pass away, as all feelings do.

The moment we take our attention off the sadness and frustration, the boredom or intolerance, they're gone. But instead we believe our feelings stay with us and act accordingly. When the feeling of anger arises, people become angry instead of saying, 'Ah yes. It's a feeling of anger. It will pass. I'll take my attention off it.' Nothing creates ego except the belief that 'I am the body. I am the feeling.'

PERCEPTIONS

Next we consist of perceptions, which tell us what things are. When the eye sees something, all it can distinguish is shape and colour. The eye can only see that this is square and white in front and black at the back. But because you've seen such a thing many times before, you know this is a clock. The mind says 'clock' and then the mind might continue, 'I wonder if it's local. She probably brought it with her from Australia. I wonder what it would cost over there?' That's the mind talking. But if a three year old comes in here and sees this, he may try playing ball with it. He doesn't know it's a clock. He might think it's a ball because he's familiar with balls, or he might think it's a building block and try to make a house with it. That's what he's familiar with. That's his perception of it.

The eye sees only shape and colour, but perception has the conditioning of memory. Somebody who hasn't got a clock might think, 'I want one like that too.' Or somebody who has a better one might think, 'Mine is much more valuable.' Ego is arising immediately, asserting its desires or superiority feelings. In reality, all we have seen is a square little box black at the back and white at the front. Because of ego delusion and conditioning, perception creates a thinking process which we, of course, believe. There's no reason to disbelieve it because we've never analysed it. By believing it, we are perpetuating the ego illusion. We are constantly thinking because we have to support our ego illusion. The ego is so fragile that it will fall apart unless it's supported. We keep adhering to the demands of the body and we *become* the feeling to support our ego illusion. If we were only to look at the feeling and say, 'It's just a feeling,' then there would be no ego affirmation.

Ego needs constant support because it isn't real. We don't have to keep saying, 'This is a house. This is a big house. This is an old house.' It's obvious. This house exists. But the ego doesn't and therefore it needs constant confirmation. This support comes from our thinking process and gets additional help from being appreciated and loved and through sense contacts and our perception of them.

MENTAL FORMATIONS

We further consist of mental formations. They are also called the kamma-formations. They are the kamma makers. The moment the thought process starts, we're making kamma. If somebody sees this clock and says, 'It's a clock. I don't have one. I'd like one too,' kamma has been made, the kamma of greed. Or someone says, 'This is a nice clock. Mine isn't as nice.' That's kamma of envy. Immediately when the thought process starts, some kamma is being made. Some of it is neutral. There's no impact from it. When one just says, 'Ah, that's a clock,' that's neutral. But most of the time we make either good or bad kamma. If we see a colour and we say, 'I'm going to paint my house that colour,' that's neutral. But behind it may already be the intention of having a nicer house than the neighbour. That's unskilful kamma.

When we believe all that's going on in the mind, we have our cherished ego support. That's why it's so difficult to stop thinking in meditation. Because the ego support would be lost. Even if the thinking stops for a moment and there is calm and quiet, the thoughts will immediately come back and say, 'Ooh, what was that? That was nice.' That's the end of that meditation and one has to start all over again. There is constant kamma being made with our thought processes. They are judging, deciding, grasping or rejecting. Only the mindfulness of moment-to-moment awareness can make a correct analysis. Then we can see what we're doing and no longer need to believe all that the mind tells us. In meditative practice one notices clearly that most of the mind-stuff is pretty unbelievable. It's either old and gone or it hasn't even happened yet. Or it's plain fantasy. Most of the thoughts that flit through the mind have no real connection with anything. The mind usually grasps at some trigger and uses it to play its own games.

SENSE CONSCIOUSNESS

The fifth attribute that we consist of is sense consciousness. This means the contact we make with our senses. The eye, the object and eye consciousness come together and what results is sight. The ear, the sound and ear consciousness together produce hearing, etc. We are constantly using our senses. At this moment you are using your eyes, your ears, your touch and your mind consciousness. The eyes see what goes on around you, the ears hear what I'm saying and the touch notices the sitting posture. The mind tries to grasp the meaning of what is heard. We try to create situations in which the senses contact what pleases us. But the endeavour is hopeless. It isn't possible to obtain only pleasant contacts. Constant attacks are being made on us through the senses. This is the way of living beings and very noticeable in the human realm.

When there is a very loud noise, people become frightened. Some noises are pleasing to us and yet if we were to continue them without end, they would become unbearable. We can't simply continue to play Beethoven for the rest of our lives.

The senses are not exactly what we think they are. In fact most people take them for granted. They don't even think about them. All they want are the pleasurable sensations. Pleasure is certainly available through the senses but very few people ever think that the senses are actually a misery to us. They are constantly pushing us in all directions trying to find pleasure from them.

The Buddha gave a simile about the body, its incessant demands and resulting misery. A father and mother are travelling through the desert with their small child. They run out of provisions but continue their journey until they become so weak and hungry that they can't go on. In the end they slay the child and eat it.

Our mental formations are compared to a prisoner who is being dragged by two fellows into a flaming pit. Our thought processes, whether good or bad, drag us into the flames of rebirth. The Buddha tried to show with these similes the inherent unsatisfactoriness of all that constitutes a human being, so that we make real effort to get out of the wheel of birth and death. We have to understand that there is no individual who owns body, feeling, perception, thought and consciousness. That is the most difficult aspect of the Buddha's teaching. Difficult to conceptualize and even more difficult to experience. Without meditation, it will remain an intellectual exercise.

Five khandhas – five aggregates – five attributes is all we are. Then the question arises, 'If that's all we are, what are we trying so hard for?' Yes, that's all we are but that's not what we think we are. We've got to work with what we know and we don't know that that's all we are. We know something entirely different about ourselves. We know this is 'me' with body and feeling, perception and thinking and sense consciousness. So we have to work with that and purify our emotions in order to come to the point where we *do* know that's all there is. When there isn't anybody there, there couldn't possibly be a problem. Problems only exist if there's somebody there to have them.

'There is the deed, but no doer. There is suffering, but no sufferer. There is the path, but no one to enter it. And there is liberation, but no one to attain it.'

11   *Ten Virtues*

Giving, virtue, then renunciation,
Wisdom and energy come to five;
Patience, truth, resolution, love,
With equanimity, these are ten.
The Buddha's words
Buddhavamsa II v. 76

There are three qualities in our make-up which help meditation: generosity, moral conduct and loving-kindness. They are not the only ones, there are others which are essential ingredients of any spiritual life and need to be cultivated.

They are called pāramīs, from parama which means supreme. We have their seed in us. If that were not so, we would be cultivating barren ground. But we do have the potential of these qualities in us, so there's something we can do. Unless we are willing to apply ourselves though, we are not going to achieve a strong and secure mind, which can be master of its own destiny. We are always going to be dependent upon the emotions and goodwill of others, upon our surroundings and our comforts. As long as we are dependent upon any or all of these, we are slaves to them. To be a slave is not a very pleasant way of living. It involves a lot of fear. Everybody has some fears, but to be dependent upon other people or outer circumstances makes it quite impossible to have freedom of thought and action. Such freedom can eventually liberate us. That doesn't mean we do what we want. Freedom of thought means a person is an independent thinker, capable of original thoughts and can determine his or her own course of action.

GENEROSITY

The spiritual qualities we need to cultivate start with generosity. The one at the top of the list is the one that opens the door. It doesn't mean that the others are less important, but unless the first one has been cultivated, that particular pathway has not opened up yet. We have to enter a path somewhere and it is the first step, or the first quality, which gives us our start.

The Buddha talked about three different kinds of generosity: the beggarly kind, the friendly kind, and the princely or kingly kind. The beggarly kind of generosity is when one gives away what one doesn't want anyway – the things that are cluttering up the house and one wants to tidy up. Giving away these things, while better than nothing, isn't very generous, because one is not diminishing one's own wants and attachments in any way.

The friendly kind of generosity is when we share what we have. We share it with as many people as come into our orbit. We give away evenly, keeping some and giving away some.

The princely kind is where we give away more than we keep. Pretty rare, isn't it? Most people don't do that.

Giving needs to have the right motivation behind it. If one gives in order to get whatever one is after – merit, appreciation, gratitude – it doesn't work. It's a contradiction in terms. One doesn't give in order to get. One gives in order to give. Only when one investigates this and inquires into it, does one see that quite clearly. If one gives in order to give, one is certain to get, namely happiness, satisfaction, peace of mind, contentment. One may give because one feels that one has more than one needs. One may give because one feels that others need to share in one's own wealth and prosperity. One may give because there's compassion in one's heart. The Buddha gave out of compassion.

Generosity doesn't only apply to giving away *things*. Not everybody has material possessions to give away, although most of us do. In fact most people have so many more belongings than they can remember, that they only find them when they come to move house. We own so many things for day to day use in the household that it would be possible to give most of them away and still have enough. But that's not the only kind of giving there is. There is the giving of one's time, one's attention, concern, care and the sharing of one's skills and abilities. That's an important giving and it's done on a large scale by governments and foreign aid agencies. But the thing that's wrong with that is, that perhaps the people who actually do the work aren't in it to practise generosity but are doing it because they are getting paid for a job, and so it is a commercial enterprise. But giving away one's skills and abilities without any thought of getting something in return is compassionate giving. The Buddha gave his Dhamma out of compassion.

That way of giving has gain in it. The more one gives out of compassion, the more compassion one necessarily has to have. It's obvious and logical, yet hardly anyone considers this aspect. Some people give to gain goodwill from others. But the more one gives out of the goodness of one's heart, the more goodness one obviously must have.

Generosity of any kind diminishes the ego and that is why it is the first of the ten virtues that need to be cultivated and protected. When the Buddha was still a Bodhisattva aiming at enlightenment, those were the qualities that he perfected and there are many stories about this in the *Jataka* tales of the Buddha's former births.

The generosity of Bodhisattvas goes as far as giving their own lives. Giving one's life for others is the greatest generosity. It is almost impossible for ordinary people to do that. But there are degrees of giving and a little giving diminishes the ego a little. A lot diminishes it a lot if the right motivation is behind it.

Diminishing the ego is the essence of the pathway to purification and leads to the eventual actual experience of non-self. One can't hope, wish or imagine that one can experience this unless one has started to do something about one's egocentricity. How would it be possible? Generosity is an excellent beginning.

MORAL CONDUCT

Next comes moral conduct, which concerns keeping the five precepts. They are directed at the diminishing and eventual overcoming of hate and greed. Diminishing hate and greed is another way of diminishing ego because they can only arise due to the ego delusion.

All the Buddha's teachings go in the same direction. Sometimes people find it confusing that there are so many different discourses in which the Buddha approached spiritual emancipation. Yet it's like a huge jigsaw puzzle. When a few of the pieces fall into place, the whole makes one matching picture. The whole of the Dhamma is directed towards first getting the ego down to manageable size and then eventually getting rid of it altogether.

Following and keeping the precepts is part of the picture. When we don't hurt living beings, hate is eliminated in our heart. We can only hurt or kill what we dislike. When we don't take what's not given we reduce greed. Only when there's greed we will take what's not ours. The same goes for sexual misconduct. Wrong speech can be due to either greed or hate. Drugs and intoxicants are most often greed for pleasant sensations which appear to be easily obtained in this way.

RENUNCIATION

Then comes renunciation. Renunciation is often thought of as being something for monks, nuns, yogis or special people who live in caves, but that is not the only way to understand it. Renunciation means renouncing one's ego aspirations and unless we do some of that during meditation, meditation will not flourish. The ego likes to be entertained and reaffirmed constantly. When it is made to be quiet and not do anything interesting, it objects quite vehemently and tries to circumvent the situation by finding something to support it, such as talking, reading, daydreaming, anything to keep it going. Unless we renounce these tendencies, meditation cannot succeed.

In the same way all the virtues are supports for meditation. All of them strengthen one's backbone. Meditation needs a strong backbone, not only for sitting straight but also for thinking straight.

Renunciation is part of any spiritual path. It means letting go of our idea of who we are or what we want to become or what we want to have. These are ego identifications which constantly reaffirm 'me,' and are going in the wrong direction. What we think we own – 'my' house, 'my' furniture, 'my' husband, 'my' wife, 'my' children, 'my' relatives, 'my' car, 'my' job, 'my' office, 'my' friends – makes the 'me' feel more secure because it constitutes a support system. It gives the ego an illusory stability. None of the people or possessions are permanent though, all are constantly on the verge of disappearing.

If there were reality to this stability then the bigger the house or the car, the more friends or children, the more wives or husbands, the more secure one would be. Yet, having all these people and things brings just more worries and problems. Imagine having ten husbands instead of one. Perish the thought! Another one of our misconceptions as to what makes us secure. What we like to surround ourselves with is the 'I,' 'me' and 'mine' making. Our concepts make it so, because obviously we can't own anyone. People die at the most inopportune moments, marry the wrong people and go away without so much as a by your leave. They make their own kamma. Yet we still call them 'mine' and actually believe them to belong to us. As soon as we believe that, then we hang on to them for dear life. They have to remain 'mine.' This is our identification process with our family, our job and the things we own. Instead of just being one 'me' we have now grown and are embedded in several people, a job, a house and all that goes with it. So we look somewhat larger.

To renounce this identification is a very important step: only if one stands alone can one actually practise the path. That doesn't mean one has to throw everyone out of one's house. But as long as one is dependent upon what somebody else says, thinks or does, how can one practise for one's own freedom? Without this identification the ego returns to its normal size, just one 'me' and that's all. It doesn't mean that the ego has been eliminated, but it has become more manageable again. One body, one mind, without owning and identifying with a whole lot of people and things.

Becoming something or someone, even an excellent meditator, is another ego affirmation. Instead of *being* right now, and being totally attentive to what there really is, one wants to *become*, which is in the future. What is there to say about the future? Nothing. The future is a complete blank. But *being*, right now, is something we can attend to with total awareness.

To become something more than what one is – an excellent meditator, a boss, famous, rich, beloved – makes the ego a bit bigger again. Becoming isn't useful, being is. That's the ego down to manageable size again. We can actually be aware of being. But we can't be aware of what we're going to become. It's not there. It's daydreaming. It's hoping and wishing. Something else we can renounce.

As part of the letting go process we can renounce our possessions, our identifications and our becoming. If we don't let go in daily living, it is very difficult to let go in meditation. In meditation we must let go of thinking, hoping, judging, expecting, desiring, comforts. We have to let go if we want to meditate, so we need to practise it at other times also. It doesn't mean we have to throw away our possessions or our family. It just means throwing away our identification with them.

Renunciation can take diverse forms. It can be self-discipline such as getting up a little earlier than usual, renouncing one's inclination to be more comfortable. Renunciation can take the form of not always eating when one feels like it, but waiting until there is real hunger. When we come to the end of life we have to renounce everything. We can't take with us any of the possessions or people we call mine, we can't even take with us the body we call mine. We might as well learn something about death before it comes. This is why the death moment is so often a struggle. Some people die peacefully, but many do not because they're not ready to renounce everything. Previously they hadn't given this any thought.

Everything we cling to is a hindrance, an obstacle. If I were to keep on clinging to this pillow here, I couldn't get out of that door. We mostly cling to other people and that needs to be renounced. It doesn't mean to get rid of the people. It means to get rid of our clinging attitude towards them, which is the biggest hindrance. Unless we take some steps in that direction, meditation is going to be hindered in the same way, because we are going to keep on clinging to our thoughts, our hopes and our wishes.

We can remain in the same house, wear the same clothes, look the same way and yet have renounced some of our strongest attachments. That doesn't mean we no longer love our family. On the contrary, love without attachment is the only kind of love that has no fear in it and is therefore pure. Love with attachment is a fetter. It consists of waves of emotion and usually creates invisible iron bands. Real love is love without clinging, it's giving without expectation, it's standing next to rather than leaning on.

WISDOM

To find the right direction in life we need the next virtue of wisdom. Its counterpart is faith. Faith and wisdom need to act together.

The Buddha compared faith to a blind giant who meets a small sharp-eyed cripple called wisdom. Faith says to wisdom, 'I'm very strong, but I can't see where I'm going. And you're very weak, but you have very good eyes. Come and ride on my shoulders. Together we'll go far.' Blind faith can move mountains, but unfortunately it doesn't know which mountain to move. Wisdom is absolutely essential to point the way. It has the sharp eye of inner vision.

Wisdom is an interesting factor because it isn't something we can learn but arises from inner purification.

Wisdom takes three steps. The first one is learning, which creates knowledge. That is available in schools, universities, colleges, books and in the words of learned people. Then we must digest those words and thereby make them part of our own inner being. When one digests food, what the body can't use is evacuated. What the body can use is fed into the bloodstream and produces energy. When we have knowledge we can do the same. We can digest it, let go of what we can't use and take the best into our bloodstream. It may eventually transform itself into wisdom, just as the digested food has transformed itself into the fuel that keeps the body running. This is an inner transformation and doesn't necessarily mean that we have to ingest or digest enormous tomes of knowledge. It's not the quantity but the quality, and even that has its parallel in food.

Chewing over and swallowing information precedes the digesting of it. Inner action is involved and this is an essential part of growth, just as physical food rightly used is essential for growth. If there is no inner action concerning the Buddha's teaching it will always belong to the Buddha and the Sangha. It will never be one's own, even though one may repeat it over and over again. Unless one has chewed, swallowed and digested the information, it cannot transform into inner wisdom.

The more wisdom we have the easier it is to lead a harmonious life without too many ups and downs. Lack of wisdom gets us into situations from which we have to extricate ourselves with a great deal of difficulty. Sometimes we might not be able to get out for some time. With wisdom we don't get into difficulties in the first place. If wisdom has faith as its support then it becomes extremely strong. The giant faith has complete confidence and cannot be shaken. When the sharp eyes of wisdom go along with it, that brings one to the goal.

Wisdom alone sometimes takes on a two-sided quality. It can see both sides of the same question or problem. It doesn't have the inner commitment that faith provides. Faith doesn't need to rest in some outer agency. A faith that does depend on an outside agency is shaky because it needs that agency to exist in a way that can be proved and can't be doubted. Nobody is allowed to cast any doubts, whatever one believes in. The most effective of faiths is faith in one's own ability to reach the highest state. In addition to that, faith may arise that one has found the right path. Here it means unshakable faith in the Dhamma together with sharp-eyed wisdom.

ENERGY

The next is energy, which one can compare to the fuel that keeps the motor running. In our case we need to generate it ourselves. It's also one of the seven factors of enlightenment, so you can see its importance.

Energy can be directed in many ways. One can expend a lot of energy in becoming a millionaire, or in building a house, or in getting the better of another person. Anything we do requires energy.

Energy can also make us restless. It can keep us running from one activity to another or from one thought to another. It can carry us from one side of the world to the other, trying to find something satisfying. It has a negative quality if it isn't used properly. It isn't wholesome in itself. It's just fuel for which we have to provide the right kind of vehicle.

The Buddha speaks about five spiritual faculties and compares them to a team of horses pulling a wagon with one lead horse and two pairs. The horse out in front is mindfulness and it can go as fast as it wishes. It doesn't have another to balance with. Mindfulness is in the lead, it is first and foremost. Without it the wagon couldn't get started. But the other two pairs have to balance with each other. The first of the two pairs is energy which has to balance with concentration.

Concentration settles one down. If there is only concentration and no energy, one becomes drowsy. One can become apathetic and lethargic. It can become concentration without mindfulness, because there isn't enough energy to be awake and aware. That kind of concentration isn't useful. It needs energy to balance with. But energy without concentration is also useless because it can make one so restless that one always has to do something.

Energy has to have a direction. It's no use putting the fuel into the vehicle, getting it started but not knowing where to go with it. That's a waste of fuel, isn't it? Since we have one energy crisis after another on this globe, it's a shame to waste any fuel, isn't it? We need to make sure we know where this vehicle of ours is going. It should have one direction only. Upwards towards growth to attain a higher, more elevated consciousness.

When one grows one gets a more expanded vision. When we grow enough we can get a bird's-eye view. When such mental and spiritual growth has been achieved and we can look down at everything from above, what is happening below no longer affects us. Whether there is a flood or a drought or even an earthquake on this globe of ours or a spaceship up in space, our consciousness won't be affected. It has a bird's-eye view of it. With that kind of view, we see the whole instead of the particular. We can, if we're up far enough in space, see the whole of this globe down below. While we're down here physically, just all we can see is this room.

The same applies to our inner vision. Our contracted vision can see only what is directly in front of it: the aches and pains of the body, the fears and worries about the future, the regrets about the past, the likes and dislikes, the people around one. That's all it can see because it doesn't have any expanded vision. But when it grows, it can see suffering as universal and it no longer bothers with worries and fears because it knows future and past to be one existence. There's only the moment.

Energy needs single-minded, one-pointed direction in order to get any results. To meditate takes a surprising amount of mental energy: the only energy in this universe. Everything physical is an outcome of mental energy. When meditation becomes skilful the expended mental energy is no longer a strain. On the contrary, the opposite happens. New energy is absorbed through meditation.

Energy is especially necessary to overcome one's instincts. Instinctual living is for animals. We are further evolved and must therefore use reflection, yet we see a lot of instinctive reactions in ourselves and others. It takes much energy to overcome them because reacting instinctively is so much part of our nature. What is absolutely natural in us – that which comes so easily – is what we need to transcend. To be an ordinary worldling means to have suffering. To transcend being an ordinary worldling means to become a noble one (*ariya*) on the way to liberation. To overcome our natural way of living and reacting as a worldling needs a lot of energy.

We need energy for anything we do. Determination gets us started but energy keeps us going. Only if we know our direction will we be able to maintain it without flagging. People who are able to do so usually accomplish much more than others and are greatly admired. There is nothing to marvel at. These are people with well-directed energy.

PATIENCE

The next is patience. If one doesn't have patience in daily living one often becomes uneasy and worried. One tries to do things which are not even effective in order to speed up the results of one's own plans.

Impatience shows up the ego because we want things to happen the way we have planned them. We also want them to happen at the time we've decided for them. Our own ideas are the only ones taken into consideration. We forget there are other factors and other people involved. We also forget we are only one of four billion people on this planet, that this planet is one little speck in this galaxy, and that there are innumerable galaxies. We conveniently forget such matters. We want things our own way *now*. When it doesn't happen according to our own preconceived notion, an impatient person usually becomes angry. It's a vicious circle of impatience and anger.

Patience has a quality of insight. One realizes that plans can be made but that anything can interfere with them. Sometimes this may even be a good or kammic result. One is willing to accept setbacks. If we can't accept what happens in our own life, we have double suffering. Everybody experiences single suffering. But when we don't accept that, the suffering at least doubles because resistance hurts. When we push against something hard enough, our hand starts to hurt. If we put our hand gently on a door or a wall there is no pain. Resisting or wanting, that's where all our suffering comes from.

The patient person is one who can see the overall event, that things change, move and flow. What seems so terrible today may seem quite all right tomorrow or next month or next year. What was so urgently required and needed a year ago makes absolutely no difference today. In this manner one pays non-judgemental attention to whatever is happening. If it isn't exactly as one had hoped it could be, all of it is looked upon as just part of the flux and the flow.

The virtues can only be cultivated to a great extent when some insight has arisen. Insight is what lies behind the cultivation of the wisdom and energy needed to go in the right direction, and the patience and renunciation needed to counteract egocentricity, because all is impermanent, unsatisfactory and substanceless.

'Insight' in Buddhist terminology always means penetration

into one of these three characteristics. They never stop their activities. The only thing that stops is our attention to them. We keep looking the other way. We don't like these three, so we resist and reject them. We deny their existence and have all sorts of ideas of how we could escape them. The only way to escape them is to accept, understand and become them, then we have escaped once and for all. Anything else is a momentary escape route that leads nowhere and brings us right back to where we started.

We need patience with ourselves. Without it we're not going to have patience with anybody else. If we get impatient with ourselves we lack appreciation of ourselves. We have exaggerated ideas about our abilities and worth and dislike it when reality doesn't comply with our ideas. We should be enlightened already, or we should be able to sit for two hours without moving, or we should go without sleep. All sorts of 'shoulds.' Such ideas are then transferred to everybody else and we become impatient with others' deficiencies.

Patience mustn't deteriorate into complacency. A very patient person has the lovely quality of being unruffled. But if there isn't enough insight and wisdom, so called patience can easily deteriorate into being complacent, thinking it doesn't matter what one does, which of course is not true. It does matter to be wholesome and skilful. One has to employ wisdom to make patience a real virtue. While accepting what is going on and seeing it as the flux and the flow, still to have the determination and the energy to redirect oneself into upward growth.

A complacent person could look at his clothes and say, 'Well, they get dirty. What is there to do? All clothes get dirty.' That's going too far. Or someone may look at their room and say, 'It is messy. All rooms get messed up.' Or someone may look at their house and say, 'The paint's come off. Well, all paint comes off.' That's letting everything happen without the determination and energy needed to redirect into an upward growth, externally and internally. One might see some defilement in oneself and say, 'Well, what's there to do? Everybody's got greed and hate,' and leave it at that. Well, that's not good enough.

On the other hand, if we do see the greed and hate in

ourselves, it's no use becoming impatient. It takes time. We've been here from time immemorial, again and again acting out greed and hatred. It will take a while to get rid of them. Patience is needed, but not complacency.

TRUTH

Now comes truth and that has many facets. First and most obviously one speaks the truth. That is the fourth precept – not to lie. But it goes much further than that. One needs to find out about oneself with real inner honesty. This is fairly difficult. It take some wisdom to find out what is wrong with oneself, not what is wrong with everybody else. It is not so difficult to find out about other people. It is fairly apparent. But to find out what is wrong with oneself, that is difficult, and needs penetrating truth and inner honesty.

It is like digging inside, questioning oneself. When the first question brings an answer that answer has to be questioned again, 'Why am I doing what I'm doing? Why am I feeling what I'm feeling? Why am I reacting the way I'm reacting?' In the end the answer will always be 'ego' if one has dug down deep enough.

The facile reactions of 'Well, it's just my ego and there's nothing I can do about it,' or 'It's just my kamma,' aren't useful. Both are equally non-productive, because if one has dug down inside oneself again and again and has seen the results of the ego assertions, then one will want to find some way of loosening the hold the ego has.

It is very difficult to see ourselves as others see us. We have to put a mirror in front of ourselves, not to see our physical shape, but to see our mental and emotional make-up. This mirror is called mindfulness. Sometimes the way other people react can create a mirror, but not a totally truthful one, because their own ego is involved. The main work has to be done by questioning oneself.

Truth has other facets. To know the truth means knowing the four noble truths and this is the true Dhamma. Knowing the four noble truths means that we have seen them with our inner vision: the noble truth of suffering; the noble truth of the cause of suffering, which is craving; the noble truth of the cessation of suffering, which is liberation; and the noble truth of the way to cessation, which is the noble eightfold path. Ultimately the word 'truth' implies just that.

All truth must in the end lead to freedom and liberation. People search for truth in many different ways, through innumerable ideologies. Some ideologies are frightening because they are concerned with oppressing one kind of person and only elevating another kind. Some are concerned with retaliation and supremacy. The human mind invents such modes of thought. Unenlightened minds base their ideologies on ego delusion, therefore none of them can bring total satisfaction.

Searching for truth is a good thing and young people *should* inquire and older people should never stop. But unfortunately the search for truth does stop. People get so caught up in the many daily responsibilities that are geared towards survival, that searching for the truth beneath all that seems beyond their capacity. They no longer have enough energy or interest. It is unfortunate that the young person doesn't have enough wisdom yet to really see the truth and the older person, who could have wisdom and experience, no longer has the energy. As Bernard Shaw said, 'Youth is wasted on the young.'

One should never let up on the search for truth, not for one moment. If one keeps on searching, one must eventually come to the realization that truth cannot be man-made. Truth must be universal. It must apply to everyone, not to certain people, certain categories, certain sexes, certain nations or religions. It has to show a way to eliminate human suffering, totally and irrevocably – not momentarily and not for a certain group only.

It has to be absolute and not relative truth. Absolute truth goes far beyond our human problems and the inquiries we usually make. It belongs to the realm of spiritual inquiry and it is on the spiritual path that absolute truth can be found. The relativity in which we live is two-dimensional. It has tomorrow and yesterday, good and bad, you and me, them and us, I want it and I don't want it, embedded in it. There is 'my' personality and 'my' individuality which 'I' like to assert and 'I' like to expand. That's relativity and that cannot be absolute truth because it cannot be satisfying to everyone. It will always be at the expense of someone else. Absolute truth has to by-pass all that. The understanding of the lack of personality and individuality may dawn and realization may arise that what is 'I,' 'me' and 'mine' has been a mistake and what has been 'you' and 'yours' an unfortunate misunderstanding. There isn't anyone to worry or to fear. All is movement and solidity is only an appearance. Absolute truth is not limited to a group or to people with a particular belief. It is universal and can be experienced through practising the noble eightfold path. The perfection of the virtues creates inner strength and to break through relative reality into absolute reality needs a lot of strength.

DETERMINATION

The next quality we need to cultivate is determination. Without it we can't accomplish anything. It even takes determination to get up in the morning, doesn't it? Some things need more determination than others, for instance meditation. In the beginning it is not all that interesting for most people to meditate, and also not comfortable. It is not very exciting and doesn't seem to bring immediate benefits.

We live in a society of instant results. Press a button, and your whole shopping list is added up. Press another button, the fan goes on and cools the air. Press another button and the light goes off or on. Everything is instant. Our society, more so than ever before, expects immediate results. That is why pain killers are far more popular than herbal remedies which take much longer to be effective.

Meditation is a slow but sure remedy. To practise it one needs determination, which is a solid character quality. A wobbly, jelly-like mind can't have much determination. A strong, resolute mind can have a lot. Every time we sit down we have to be determined to stay there, not to wriggle around, to keep the mind in its place, to really attend to what we are doing.

Determination is also needed in everyday living. If we wait for things to happen, it is highly unlikely that they will. We have to do something about them. It took determination for you to come to this meditation course. It would have been more comfortable at home.

We have all these character qualities within us. We certainly have the quality of moral conduct. If most people didn't have that, the world would be in much greater chaos than it is already. We certainly have the virtue of determination, but we don't have the deep-seated wisdom that these qualities are our best friends. We must try to be near them, keep them with us and make them grow. They are necessary ingredients for a happy and peaceful life and are indispensable for spiritual progress.

That is really all life can offer us: spiritual progress. Aside from that, there are only momentary pleasures. These are dangerous because they lull us into complacency. When we see this with clarity, then the determination arises to make spiritual progress our priority. We need not live in a monastery or a cave for that. We can make progress or backslide anywhere. Whatever happens is used as a teaching aid, whether it is sickness or death, whether it is ill-will or the loss of possessions, physical discomfort and pain or love and fame. Attachment to other people and worry about them are a teaching aid. Take nothing for granted but use everything in order to grow.

Determination arises when we can see that life has nothing else of value to offer, except our own spiritual growth and final emancipation. We need not change our lifestyle but our approach, our reactions and our understanding of what is happening around and within ourselves. That kind of determination brings happiness because with it comes the joy of the path. Determination is then self-regenerating. Ordinary determination arises and ceases and a struggle ensues to make it come to life again. But when the determination is the determination of the spiritual path, it need not be re-aroused over and over. It stays because it creates joy.

LOVING-KINDNESS AND EQUANIMITY

You've already heard about the last two virtues. They are mentioned here again: loving-kindness and equanimity.

Equanimity is the crowning glory of all emotions. It necessitates the loss of ego illusion. If we have no inkling of the fact that the ego creates all the hustle and turmoil, we cannot develop real equanimity. We may suppress anxiety and restlessness, but we cannot feel even-minded. Insight and wisdom must lie at the base of equanimity.

These ten virtues are developed life after life, again and again, until they become strong enough to effect a breakthrough onto the noble path where we can have an inner vision of the four noble truths at the hub of the wheel of Dhamma.

12   *The Four Noble Truths and the Noble Eightfold Path*

When the Buddha left home to find the answer to the suffering of humanity, he went to two well-known meditation teachers. The first, Ālāra Kālāma, taught him the first four meditative absorptions, the meditative absorptions of the form realm. He was an excellent student and learned very quickly. Soon his teacher told him to take over the teaching because he was just as capable as the teacher himself. But the Buddha, who was still Prince Siddhartha Gotama at that time, refused and said that he had not achieved his goal yet and left to study with Uddaka Rāmaputta, his second teacher. Uddaka Rāmaputta taught him the four formless absorptions which are more refined and more concentrated than the first four absorptions of the form realm. Again he was an excellent student and the teacher told him to take over all his disciples. Again the prince refused because he realized that even though he was able to go into the highest meditative absorption, when he came out of this meditation, the suffering situation was the same as before. Nothing much had changed. Since Uddaka Rāmaputta said he could teach him nothing further, the prince knew that he now had to strike out on his own. He left the five ascetics who had been his friends. They didn't want to accompany him but preferred the safety and security of having an established teacher.

When the prince came to the Bodhi tree in what today is Bodhgaya in northern India he made a resolution. He would sit there without moving and without getting up even if his flesh should rot from the bones. So he sat and used the meditation skills he had learned to go into deep concentration from the first to the eighth meditative absorption, and back down again. While he was sitting there he was beset by Māra, temptation, which he successfully resisted. As his mind was totally calm and concentrated, not a ripple, not a movement, it was possible for him to gain the deepest insight. When he came out of this deep absorption, he could see the four noble truths and the noble eightfold path as an inner reality which left no residue. After he had done so, he realized he had become the Buddha, the fully Enlightened One.

He sat in the bliss of liberation offering great gratitude to the Bodhi tree which had sheltered him. He stayed there for a month but upon the pleas of the highest god, Brahma Sahampati, he decided that he would teach. At first, he thought that his teaching would be too profound, too difficult to understand. Trying to impart it to people, he would be vexed by their lack of comprehension. But he relented and agreed to teach for the benefit of humans and gods.

First he wanted to help his own teachers. When he tried to find them with his clairvoyant vision, he saw they had already died. Then he decided to teach his friends in the holy life, the five ascetics, who had studied with him. He looked to see where they were and found them near Benares. He decided to go and meet them there.

He walked the whole way. During his forty-five years of teaching ministry, he walked everywhere. He never took a vehicle because in those days vehicles were pulled by animals and he would not burden an animal with his weight. Therefore, it is one of the rules for monks and nuns not to use an animal-drawn vehicle. We are lucky today, having other kinds of vehicles. The Buddha always walked.

He taught every day. That's why such a wealth of material is available to us. In the original texts there exist over 17,500 discourses.

When he got near Benares, the five ascetics saw him coming. They said to each other, 'Look who's coming. Master Gotama. He has deserted the spiritual life. He's no longer an ascetic. He's well fed, clean shaven. We're not even going to greet him when he comes near.' But their resolution was soon discarded because when he came nearer they were overwhelmed by the majesty of his bearing and the radiance of his face. They greeted him very politely.

Then the Buddha told them, 'I have become the Buddha and I will teach you my doctrine.' They were surprised and replied, 'But how will we know that this is truly so? How can we tell?' He said 'You've known me for six years. Have I ever deceived you?' They said, 'No.' The Buddha then said, 'Give me a hearing.' They agreed to do that. In other words, they would give him the benefit of the doubt. They prepared a seat for him in the deer park of Isipatanna outside Benares and there they stayed for a week. Every day one of them went out for almsfood.

The Buddha then proceeded to proclaim his very first discourse after his enlightenment – 'the turning of the wheel of Dhamma discourse.' He started to turn the wheel of the Dhamma with that discourse and it's still turning today, which is very fortunate for us. There are times in the world cycles when there is no Dhamma and it is often endangered. There have been times during this Dhamma period when, for instance, there wasn't a single monk here in Sri Lanka. The Dhamma is always in danger of disappearing because it goes against the grain of human instinct. It goes against the stream, against the current.

As the Buddha came to the end of his Dhamma discourse, one of his listeners became enlightened. The Buddha said, 'Añña Kondañño sees, Añña Kondañño knows.' Seeing *and* knowing. It is not enough to know. Seeing means the inner vision, the inner reality, which changes one's whole outlook and attitudes. Añña Kondañño was the first Arahant and also the first Buddhist monk.

The Buddha is also called an Arahant: '*Namo tassa bhagavato arahato sammā sambuddhassa.*' He is an Arahant but he is also the Buddha. The difference being that the Buddha finds the four noble truths and the noble eightfold path by himself without any teacher, whereas the Arahant becomes enlightened by following the Buddha. When the Buddha's teaching is no longer in existence, then after many aeons a new Buddha arises finding exactly the same four noble truths and the noble eightfold path by himself. The Buddha is one who is able to expound the Dhamma. This is said to be a rare gift. There are those who are called Paccekabuddha. They are enlightened but they do not have the gift of teaching.

When one reads the discourses, one is amazed how often the Buddha repeats exactly the same words. Although it sounds very melodious in Pali, it is extremely repetitive and one wonders why. But it's not surprising. The spoken word is often repetitive. Not only that, but the Buddha realized the difficulty of penetrating to a profound truth by listening and therefore emphasized through repetiton.

THE FOUR NOBLE TRUTHS

The four noble truths start out with the noble truth of suffering. The five friends to whom he was speaking had been ascetics for six years, mortifying their bodies. The Buddha had done the same, but had found this didn't bring enlightenment. Neither had indulgence, which he experienced in his princely life in the palace, brought happiness. He realized now that there was only one way – the middle path. There are no extremes one can use to advantage. These ascetics had used mortification of the body for some time. They knew all about the suffering of the body. The Buddha didn't have to emphasize it very much. They could see it easily.

For us it's not quite so easy. Although we do feel the suffering of the body in the meditation practice, we are well aware of the fact that once we go home we are not going to have it to the same extent. This then is temporary suffering, and because it has a very definite limit we can cope with it. We're not so sure yet that this body not only *has* suffering but *is* suffering. In fact one can say that *having* this body is *suffering*. Just being burdened with a body of this kind is suffering. That doesn't mean that we are constantly beset by tragedy. Tragedy is one thing, the truth of suffering is another. The Buddha said:

> birth is suffering
> decay is suffering
> death is suffering
> not getting what one wants is suffering

These are the main aspects, but then there are the others which arise between birth, decay, disease and death. We obviously have our good days when we aren't aware there is suffering in us. We may be sorry for someone who is suffering at the time, but we're also glad that we're not experiencing it, forgetting that suffering is there all the time. It exists even in pleasure because we can't make pleasure last. Pleasure vanishes just when we want to catch hold of it. Every time we want to keep it, it disappears and we have to find it again. This body of ours cannot even sustain life unless it is constantly fed, cleaned, exercised and repaired. All sorts of repairs are necessary: glasses, teeth, hearing aids, tonics, vitamins, cough syrup, shampoos, powders and lotions. Millions of pounds are spent just to keep the body going, not even to improve it. One can't make it any younger even though many people try. All this effort, energy, money and time is expended just to keep the body functioning. Unless we do expend this effort, the body will completely disintegrate. We might not even be able to use it any more. Its inherent nature of not listening to our pleas for youth, health, beauty, long life, but doing exactly the opposite can certainly be regarded as suffering.

The greatest suffering of the body is its many demands which most people spend all their lives trying to satisfy. All the money people make, all the work they do is to keep the body intact and satisfied. They have to work to get food, a house, clothing and medicine. We wouldn't need any of that if we didn't have a body. Most people spend a lot of time trying to get a little more comfort and satisfaction for the body. That seems to be the greatest suffering – to spend one's life in this manner.

The body is not the only sufferer. The mind is too, and haven't we noticed that? It won't listen, will it? It does what it pleases, instead of staying right where we want it. It continues to think about things which have a tendency to make us unhappy. If that isn't suffering what is? It's also foolishness. But that too is suffering, isn't it?

The mind flits from one thought to another. The thinking process as such is suffering, even wholesome and skilful thoughts have an inherent disquiet in them. When there is thinking of any kind there cannot be any real calm.

The mind with its thinking and the body with its many parts are both suffering. The Buddha said there is only one cause, one reason we experience suffering, and that's craving. We have three cravings and all others are connected with them. These three are craving for existence, craving for self-annihilation and craving for sensual gratification. With these three cravings we are obviously enmeshed in suffering because all three are impossible to fulfil. There's no way we can win. We are engaged in a hopeless struggle, and *that* is real suffering.

We are engaged in the struggle for existence and yet none of us is going to exist after our time has run out. We're also engaged in the struggle for sensual gratification, and that too is hopeless because it is momentary. It can't last. The third one, the desire for self-annihilation, is the opposite of the desire for existence and arises when things look too bleak. It also can't be fulfilled because non-existence is an impossibility except for the Enlightened Ones who perceive that nobody exists.

The first and second noble truths show us that we are living a life of futility. No matter how nice our thoughts are, they are also going to perish. If one sees quite clearly that our cravings cannot possibly be gratified, then comes the moment of trying to find the way out of this dilemma which confronts every human being. Nobody is exempt. Seeing this creates compassion in our hearts for everyone, no matter how nasty, how unlovable or how stupid they are. There is no loop-hole but there is a way out.

The way out leads inward. If we check, we can't find anything outside ourselves. Most people look for a solution out there somewhere, through better conditions, nicer people, less work, a little less suffering. If we can really see the futility of that, we won't look out there any more. Instead we'll look inside and that will eventually lead to the third noble truth, the cessation of suffering which is liberation.

The Buddha never really explained what liberation *is*. He did say what it is *not*. He knew it was not useful to explain it, because nobody who hadn't experienced it would understand. It was possible to say what liberation was not because at least people wouldn't then look in the wrong direction.

The following story illustrates this. Once there were a fish and a turtle who were friends. They had been living in the same lake together for some time. One day the turtle decided to visit the land surrounding the lake. She had a good look around and came back to tell her friend the fish of the wonders she had seen. The fish was very interested and asked the turtle what it was like on land. The turtle answered that it was very beautiful. The fish then wanted to know whether it had been transparent, cool, rippling, shiny, smooth, good for gliding, buoyant and wet. When the turtle said it had none of these attributes, the fish said, 'What can be beautiful about it then?'

THE NOBLE EIGHTFOLD PATH

The way to the cessation of all suffering, which is liberation or freedom, is the fourth noble truth, the noble eightfold path. This path, like all of the Buddha's teachings, is divided into three parts: moral conduct, concentration and wisdom.

People often think that it has to go in that order, as if it were a ladder where the lowest rung of moral conduct makes it possible to get some concentration which itself leads to insight and then wisdom.

The noble eightfold path proves this incorrect. It doesn't start out with moral conduct. It starts out with wisdom. The noble eightfold path has to be looked upon, not as a ladder but as an eight-lane highway on which one has to use all lanes. It's also a circular movement because it starts out and ends with right view. Although right view is only mentioned at the beginning, the result of treading the noble eightfold path will be absolute right view.

Right View

Right view is the first step because it means that one has seen clearly that there is nothing else to be done in one's life except to find the way out of suffering through a spiritual discipline. Then one is obviously going to look for the right kind of discipline, which needs to expound what is wrong with us. Our problems are suffering, dissatisfaction, anxiety, a feeling of not being fulfilled. There is an empty spot in the heart which one constantly tries to fill with a person or several persons, an idea, a project, a hope. Nothing will fill it. When a discipline is able to expound the basic dissatisfaction that we have and then also can explain the way to eliminate that dissatisfaction and come to total contentment, one can judge that this is a reliable teaching. The teaching must also go into the complete depth of human experience. The Buddha's Dhamma is such a teaching.

Right view includes the realization that it is possible for every one of us to actually start practising. Right view also means having an understanding of kamma, namely taking full responsibility for what happens to oneself, not blaming others, or circumstances or anything outside oneself. It means taking full responsibility for what one is and where one finds oneself, and realizing that one is master of one's own destiny. One can change.

Knowing that one can change is not enough; also that one needs to change. These are two right views: the understanding of kamma and of the need to effect a change in oneself in order to get out of suffering. Not changing the world or its inhabitants or the people we happen to live with, but changing ourselves. We cannot eliminate problems but we can eliminate our own reactions. We can also eventually come to the end of the path which culminates in the right view of self, namely non-self.

Wisdom is needed to begin one's spiritual discipline. Without having had the wisdom to know that something needed to be done, we would not have started our meditation practice.

Human beings have this wonderful opportunity because of suffering. Instead of constantly resisting dissatisfaction, trying to sweep it under the carpet or lament and grieve about it and be pained by it, we should be grateful for it. It's our very best teacher. In fact you might say it is our only teacher, but unfortunately not everybody learns from it.

There are several ways of reacting to suffering. The first and common way is to blame someone else. That's the easy way. Everybody plays that game and it's childish. The second way of reacting to pain and dissatisfaction is to become depressed and get bogged down by it, indulging in unhappiness. The third reaction is being sorry for oneself, having the idea that one has all the suffering in the world. Nobody else has anything comparable, which is obviously untrue. When one is feeling sorry for oneself, one also expects others to commiserate. It doesn't work. Nothing is learned. Nothing is gained. On the contrary, one becomes a burden to others. Another way of reacting to suffering, is to grit one's teeth, suppress the emotions and pretend it hasn't happened. That too doesn't work, because pretending never works.

There is a fifth method and that is looking suffering squarely in the face and saying, 'Aha. My old friend's here again. What am I supposed to learn this time?' *That* is right view. Then we have really understood why the human realm is the best realm for enlightenment. Suffering is our best teacher because it hangs on to us and keeps us in its grip until we have learned that particular lesson. Only then does suffering let go. If we haven't learned our lesson, we can be quite sure that the same lesson is going to come again, because life is nothing but an adult education class. If we don't pass in any of the subjects, we just have to sit the examination again. Whatever lesson we have missed, we'll get it again. That's why we find ourselves reacting to similar situations in similar ways many times. However, a time does come when we notice this and the right view arises, 'I've got to do something about myself. I'm having the same problem over and over again.'

Right view is the essential foundation for entering into the spiritual path. Right view in the beginning doesn't apply to right view of self. That is the end of the path. It is basically concerned with the first two noble truths. When we see clearly that we are fighting a losing battle so long as we keep trying to have sense pleasures and protect ourselves from losing our ego, then we're on the way. That's the moment of entering the path, and it's a moment of joy. With it a certainty arises that the way out has been found and that the final result must come. It's just a matter of time. That joyous feeling is essential for meditation and meditation is essential for treading the path.

Each one of us proves the Buddha's words. We have suffering and we have craving, we have some right view and we experience kamma and its results. We can also change and we have learned something from the past suffering. We can prove the Buddha's words in many ways if we just pay enough attention. That creates self-confidence, knowing one really can tread the noble eightfold path to its very end. This confidence is necessary as part of the practice. Self-confidence is not a feeling of superiority, but of independence. We have to work independently for our emancipation.

The Buddha said that we shouldn't believe what he says but should inquire into it and verify it for ourselves. He gave ten reasons for not following a spiritual path in one of his very famous discourses, the Kālāma discourse. It applies to us today as vividly as it appeared to the Kālāma people. It is just as pregnant with meaning for us as it was then.

The Kālāma people came to see the Buddha when he visited their capital of Kesaputta and said to him, 'Sir, we have had many spiritual teachers visit our town and each one has been able to propound his teaching in an excellent, very believable way. Equally, though, everyone of these teachers denied and negated every other teacher. Now we are totally confused. We do not know whom to believe.' The Buddha said, 'It is proper for you, Kālāmas, to doubt, to be uncertain.' He then propounded the five precepts to them and asked whether they would be conducive to happiness if they were kept and conducive to unhappiness for themselves and others, if they were transgressed. The Kālāmas agreed that this would be so. Then the Buddha said to them, 'Never believe any spiritual teaching because it is repeatedly recited; or because it is written down in the scriptures; or because it has been handed down from teacher to disciple; nor because everybody around you believes it; nor because it has metaphysical qualities; nor because it agrees with what you believe anyway; nor because you can rationalize it. Don't believe it if it is a viewpoint which you need to defend and don't believe it because the teacher is a reputable person or because the teacher said so.'

When the Kālāma people had heard the Buddha, they became his followers. Here was a guideline for them, which is equally valid today. Don't believe something because it's a tradition, or because everybody around you does it, or because it's written in a book, but only, the Buddha said, if you have inquired into it and found it to be useful and true.

There's no question that we can find suffering in ourselves, and the more we look inward the more dissatisfaction will we find. When we no longer crave to change our personal suffering into personal satisfaction, with the resistance gone, the suffering goes. Acceptance of things as they are constitutes right view.

The Brahmins, the priest caste in India, were not very friendly towards the Buddha because he was undermining their livelihood. He preached that one didn't need an intermediary between oneself and the gods in order to gain happiness, also that it wasn't very useful to pour ghee over stone gods and offer flowers and incense. Since this was the livelihood of the Brahmins, although many of them did eventually become followers of the Buddha, there were others who disliked him thoroughly.

One day one of the Brahmins who objected to the Buddha came to listen to one of the Buddha's discourses and, while he was still speaking, walked up and down in front of him. Then he proceeded to abuse the Buddha, using quite rough language. He said the Buddha was the teacher of a wrong doctrine, that he should be chased out of the country, that he was breaking up family life because the young men were following him into monkhood, that the people should not support him; he reviled him in every possible way he could think of.

When he had finally run out of words the Buddha, who had been quietly sitting there listening, said, 'Brahmin, do you ever have guests in your house?' The Brahmin answered, 'Yes, of course we have guests in our house.' The Buddha said, 'When you have guests in your house, do you offer them hospitality? Do you offer them food and drink?' The Brahmin said, 'Well, of course we do. Of course I offer them food and drink.' The Buddha continued, 'And if they don't accept your hospitality, if they don't take your food and drink, to whom does it belong?' The Brahmin said, 'It belongs to me. It belongs to me.' The Buddha said, 'That's right, Brahmin. It belongs to you.'

This is a good story to remember. Any abuse, anger or threat belongs to the one who is uttering it. We don't have to accept it.

Right Intention

The second step on the noble eightfold path is right intention. Right intention comes from right view. If there is wrong view, obviously the wrong intention will follow. So it is important that we do something about our views. All our views are tainted with our ego delusion. We see things from the standpoint of 'I'm seeing' and therefore even views which are obviously not wrong in the worldly sense, are wrong in the spiritual, liberating sense. However, we have to start where we are. It's no use waiting until the day deeper understanding arrives. It won't come, anyway, unless we work for it.

Peace and happiness are not our birthright. Those who have gained them have done so through constant effort. This effort is directed towards setting one's views right so that the intention becomes right. Right view and right intention consitute the wisdom aspect of the path.

Before the Buddha became enlightened, when he was still a Bodhisattva, he watched his mind-moments carefully and realized that when he had thoughts of ill-will, thoughts of cruelty or desire, they were to his own detriment. When he had thoughts of renunciation, loving-kindness, compassion and harmlessness, they were to his own benefit. Having trained his mind sufficiently he was able to let go of thoughts which were unwholesome.

There are three aspects, then, to right intention: renunciation, loving-kindness and harmlessness. Renunciation cannot be accomplished either through wishful thinking or suppression. Neither will work. It has to be accomplished through the right view, that desire is always suffering. If we can actually experience that in ourselves, then naturally we will want to renounce the desire which has arisen. We will do so happily, joyously experiencing the real relief of having let go of suffering and problems.

Desire is always suffering because it only arises when there's something missing that we want. Whether it is food or enlightenment doesn't matter. It's something we don't have, so we desire it and experience the lack as painful. Then if we can't get what we desire, of course, there is frustration, resentment, grief, sadness. Obviously we suffer if we can't get what we want.

If we do have a particular desire gratified, that too creates disturbance in us because we know from past experience that the gratification will not last. We worry about how to prolong the pleasure. The worry is suffering and when it doesn't last, there is suffering again.

Trying to make anything last creates tension and fear. We're afraid of losing certain people, situations, belongings and feelings. There is also the fear of not getting them when we want them, such as arises after a good meditation. 'Oh, isn't this nice. Finished! I wonder if I could have that again? What am I going to do now?' Suffering has arisen, because any desire has this as its feature. Only when we recognise this in ourselves with certainty, will we be able to start renouncing. It's our attachment to things and people that we want to keep which creates suffering for us. Nothing but pain and problems until life's end. Unless we know it, we won't be able to give it up.

Renunciation starts when one gives something away that one knows one is really attached to. If one can do that happily, not with teeth clenched and eyes closed so that one won't see what's going on, but joyously, then one has seen the danger of clinging.

More important than giving things away is giving up one's views and opinions about oneself and the world and about how other people should behave and react, especially those one is close to. All this is suffering, being bound up in the desire for having and owning.

There's also the desire for *being*, being loved for instance. Or being a wife and mother, or being famous or being appreciated. Any desire is suffering and prevents one from feeling contented and peaceful. To be different from how one is, is another desire that creates suffering. To work and gently transform oneself is different. But desires in the mind are due to feeling a gap, a lack, something missing. That's painful. Only renunciation can assuage that pain. We're always trying to answer that pain by trying to get what we desire. It has never killed the pain, because when desire is not renounced, it constantly reminds us of the pain.

Renunciation underlies right intention. Love and compassion and harmlessness towards other beings and our understanding of the truth of suffering bring our intentions in line. All four noble truths are bound up with each other because they go to the depth of our psyche. When we understand correctly, we can act skilfully. The suffering we have in ourselves is manifested innumerable times in all beings.

If we watch a bird, for instance. Instead of thinking what pretty feathers it has and how melodious a song, how it can fly through the air without any difficulty and go anywhere it chooses, take a better look. The bird is constantly looking around, turning its head right and left out of fear that another animal may attack it or its nest. At other times, the mating instinct comes to the fore. Then the desire for survival manifests in its constant search for food. And this is just one living being out of so many.

Look at other people and watch their faces. They don't need to say anything. And of course, watch yourself. The Buddha recommended that we get to know our internal and external world. This is mindfulness, being awake and aware. If we can see suffering in all the living beings that we contact, then we can assume, without any doubt, that it's true for all living beings, wherever they are. Unless our minds become imbued with that, loving-kindness and compassion won't flourish. There will always be some objection in the back of the mind, 'Yes, I could love her if only she wouldn't speak like this or react like that.' Or, 'I would have compassion for her, but she brought it all on herself.' None of this matters. Suffering is universally inside all of us and unless we can see that clearly, loving-kindness and compassion are going to be an off and on affair. When things go well we can manage. When things become difficult, we can't. Right intention means that we are always on the alert to act and react skilfully. It must not depend on whether we are feeling fine or whether the person is behaving in a way we can tolerate, or whether it's gone beyond that limit.

Right intention is our kamma-making process because our mental formations are having the intentions. Right view can be established in ourselves through some wisdom and insight. It will be a foundation for our intentions. Intentions are constantly arising with every action and reaction. 'Kamma, O monks, I declare, is intention,' are the Buddha's words. This is how we make kamma, and if we believe that good kamma is essential for our well-being, we have to watch our intentions.

An interesting aspect of intentions is that they are like icebergs: one-third out of water, two-thirds under water. We can only see their tips. We give something and we see the generosity, but have we examined the intention behind that generosity? In order to get to know oneself, one needs to probe into unknown depths. There are many hidden crevices inside oneself. We don't like to look, because we meet the not-so-nice aspects of ourselves. But that's why we are human beings, otherwise we might have wound up in the deva realm. We might as well acknowledge our failings. Only what we bring out into the light to see, can we clean up. The dirt under the carpet never gets cleaned unless we take the carpet away. The Buddha compared our defilements to wet hay. If it's kept in a closed barn, it will rot. But let the light of day shine on it, it will soon dry out and become useful fodder. Let's look into the hidden crevices and thoroughly examine our intentions.

The next three steps on the noble eightfold path concern moral conduct: right speech, right action and right livelihood. The first two are concerned with the precepts, divided into speech and action.

Right Speech

Speech is very important and needs a little more attention than it usually gets. Just because we know how to speak doesn't mean that we really have the skill of speech. I don't mean we should become orators. That's a different kind of skill.

The Buddha said something very interesting about speech which is well worth remembering 'If you know anything that's hurtful and untrue, don't say it. If you know anything that's helpful and untrue, don't say it. If you know anything that is hurtful and true, don't say it. If you know anything that is helpful and true, find the right time.' This means to desist from impetuous speech. We need to think about it first, to make sure that it will be helpful, that it's also true and that the right time has come. The right time has come when the other person is agreeable to listening and in a peaceful frame of mind. And it should, above all, be a time when oneself has only loving feelings for the other person. Only then should one say anything. If there is any dislike, resistance or rejection in one's mind about the other person it's going to show in the speech and it will not be useful or profitable. Everybody has occasions when they want to tell others what they should or shouldn't do. By using the above criteria, one has a good chance of success.

Right speech is traditionally explained as no slander, no gossip, no backbiting, not setting one person against another, not using harsh or abusive speech. The Buddha said that speech makes and breaks families and friends. It is at the root of harmonious companionship and also its opposite, enmity. The Buddha also said that right speech includes not overrating or understating. This means one does not exaggerate into making either maximum or minimum statements. That too is lying. It's based upon the wish to make oneself a little more interesting.

When the Buddha's son Rāhula was seven years old, the Buddha delivered an exhortation to him. In it he talks to his son about not lying, which is so important for children and adults alike. He wouldn't have given that discourse to his own son had he not thought it crucial to Rāhula's development. He showed him a pitcher with a little water in it and said to him, 'What do you see, Rāhula?' The little boy answered, 'I see only a little water.' The Buddha said, 'So little as this water in here is the trustworthiness of a person who lies.' Then he tipped the water out and said, 'And what do you see now?' Rāhula said, 'Well, the pitcher is empty.' The Buddha said, 'That's right. Empty is a person who lies.' Then he turned the pitcher upside down and said, 'And what do you see now, Rāhula?' Rāhula said, 'The pitcher is turned upside down.' The Buddha said, 'That's right. A person who lies turns their life upside down.'

Lying is the beginning stage of breaking all the other pre-cepts. Lying is done sometimes for self-protection, sometimes out of greed, to get more than one's due and sometimes out of hate, when one lies in order to hurt. All the reasons for lying bring us onto a downward spiral.

Speech is based on thoughts and if we have any control over our thoughts, we learn to have control over our speech. We become mindful of everything we think and learn to change it from the unwholesome to the wholesome. Unless we learn that about speech, we're not going to have many friends.

On the other hand, speech must be meaningful. Idle chatter is also wrong speech. Just talking with nothing to say, such as talking about one's family, food, the weather or how one feels. Talking as an entertainment, as a way of passing the time. Unless one becomes mindful and knows what one is saying, one should keep quiet and try to find out what one is thinking.

Right speech is one of the thirty-eight blessings in the Great Blessings discourse. It's a great blessing to be endowed with kind and polite speech, but always with meaning and right intention behind it. Two people may actually say exactly the same thing, but their intentions are different, so their kamma will be different. We will only get to know our intentions if we practise looking inward, and we can't do that while talking.

Refraining from false speech, the fourth precept needs to be examined, as to what it means in our own life. If we really want to follow the Buddha's teaching, then that precept takes pride of place, because everybody talks most of the day. When we use really meaningful speech, people will listen. When it is kindly speech, people will be joyful. When it is polite, we will be able to have many friends. When there is truthfulness, we can be relied upon. When there is no slander or backbiting, we will be trusted. We can discuss our problems and secrets with other people. If we become such a person, we will have many friends and a harmonious life, because nothing is in our mind which we need to hide. We need not worry about what and how we are going to speak and whether we have spoken correctly. Our speech will come easily because the right intention is behind it.

The Buddha also spoke about expounding the Dhamma. This should be precise, which means that one knows what one is thinking and experiencing. This is important. Anyone who speaks Dhamma, even just about one's own meditation, must be precise. This means that the mind is uncluttered and therefore precise speech can ensue. These are skills which we can learn through mindfulness. They're not to be learned through elocution lessons.

Right Action

Right action is again based on right intention. If the right intention arises, based on right view, then right action will follow. All are kamma-making because all result from intention. Speech is based on intention. Action is based on intention. All of it is kamma-making – good, bad or neutral – and not just for the next life, it is mainly for right now. Kamma and its results are constantly happening every moment. Unless one pays full attention to the results, one doesn't know that they are directly related to what one has said, thought and done.

Right action concerns the non-harming of others in any manner or form and the renouncing of cruelty and greed. To suppress cruelty and greed isn't possible. They will come up in some other way. They require letting go, which is something we need to practise in meditation. Unless we let go of our desires in meditation, there will be no meditation. There will be thinking, hoping, wishing, worrying, fearing, remembering. Unless we learn to let go of these mind states, we won't meditate. Meditation *is* renunciation, renunciation of all that roams around the mind, trying to reaffirm ego or gratifying desires. Because we haven't practised renunciation very much, it's difficult to meditate, but with continued application it becomes easier. Suppression doesn't work but renunciation of the desire to think, remember and plan brings the most excellent results. Letting go of desire is the only way to peace, and *that* experience brings with it the understanding that renunciation of desire in daily life will bring happiness.

Right action can be done under any circumstances by anyone at any time, be it in the household or at work or in a monastic situation. Wherever, whoever we are, all of us are performing some actions. We can check, whether they are beneficial for others and for ourselves. Even cooking or cleaning a floor must be done with the right intention, not because one has to do it or because it's expected or because somebody would get angry otherwise. The main reason for doing something is because it is needed at that time and one can fulfil a purpose. Watching carefully and mindfully one becomes aware of one's intentions and views. One sees the connection between mind and body, and does not consider external things. There is no resistance or reluctance, but one acts wholeheartedly. Only then does any action bring benefits.

It's often thought that work is an unpleasant interruption of one's leisure time. This is obviously wrong thinking. Leisure can be an unpleasant interruption of work. Work is a means to be useful and purposeful, no matter what kind of work one does. It is a means of paying full attention to the body and knowing its actions, its movements. It is an opportunity to help, to be of service, to gain skills and to show love by working for others. There is hardly anything that is comparable to work as a means for purification. Not just doing something to earn a living or because others expect it, but with one's whole heart as a means of seeing clearly.

Right Livelihood

Earning one's living is one of the three aspects of moral conduct: right livelihood. It means that one does not earn one's living by anything that could hurt other beings. Everybody has to come to terms with that by themselves. There are many livelihoods which are 'right,' far more than 'wrong' ones, but there are some that are hurtful. They are to be checked out against the five precepts. If one breaks any of the five precepts through one's activities, it is obviously wrong.

Right livelihood is important as an aspect of purification, because if one pursues wrong livelihood, one becomes hardened and set in a groove of unwholesome action. A killer of animals, in an abattoir, for instance, will have to deaden his compassion in order to continue that kind of work. Otherwise it is hardly likely that he could go on with it. Such a person would become hardened and would lack love and compassion for other beings.

Killing is one aspect of wrong livelihood. There is also lying, drinking intoxicants and taking what is not one's own. All these can happen as livelihoods. Wrong conduct in sexual matters can also be used as livelihood. Any one of these is quite clearly detrimental to one's own and others' well-being and based on greed. People do rationalize, justify and excuse them. If they do, that's their own view. Every step on the way depends upon right view and that is why it stands at the head of the path.

The last part of the noble eightfold path concerns concentration. It also has three factors involved: right effort, right mindfulness and right concentration. All are necessary for concentration to arise. Again, all of them are dependent upon right view. If there is right view that effort is necessary, it will arise. Mindfulness needs the right view of being an essential aspect of the spiritual path. Concentration needs the right view that it is skilful means.

Right Effort

Effort and energy have a symbiotic relationship. With energy, effort arises. They help each other. If one has no energy, obviously one can't make any effort. If one keeps on making effort, energy comes. Energy is the fuel for effort and vice versa. Effort goes against our grain, because it seems to counteract comfort. Effort and comfort are considered to be contradictory and yet, when the meditation, through effort, comes to the point of absorption one realizes that the effort that one has made has resulted in a great deal of comfort.

The Buddha recommended the four supreme efforts as skilful means. They are called 'supreme' because they are supremely difficult and supremely beneficial. They are worded like this: 'Not to let an unwholesome thought arise, which has not yet arisen. Not to let an unwholesome thought continue, which has already arisen. To make a wholesome thought arise, which has not yet arisen. To make a wholesome thought continue, which has already arisen.'

One needs to watch one's mind states and be able to distinguish wholesome from unwholesome. This is one of the reasons why I have instructed you to label your thoughts when they arise in meditation practice. Only when we know what we are thinking are we able to do something about it. Unless we know whether our mind is engaged in wholesome or unwholesome thinking, unless we can give a very distinctive label, how are we going to follow the Buddha's injunction of not letting unwholesome thoughts arise and not letting them continue, to make wholesome thoughts arise and make them continue?

Not to let unwholesome thoughts arise needs a great deal of mindfulness because one has to become aware of the thought intention. It is much easier to know what has already arisen. We need to start with what has already arisen, until we gain the skill of knowing that something unwholesome is creeping up on us and refuse to let it in.

In meditation every thought is useless because we don't want to think, but want to meditate. In daily living that's not the case. The unwholesome thoughts are the ones to get rid of. It's useless trying to suppress them. We can either drop them or we can substitute the wholesome for the unwholesome thought. In meditation we learn to substitute the thought with attention on the meditation subject. How well we can do this in meditation will reflect directly upon how well we will be able to handle the four supreme efforts in daily living. How well we can work with the four supreme efforts in daily living will reflect directly upon our meditation practice. Unwholesome thoughts in daily living reflect in restlessness and disquiet in the meditation. Wholesome thoughts continually kept and never deviated from will result in peace and quiet in the mind.

If we remember nothing else about the Buddha's teaching but the four supreme efforts, that is enough. Everything else that we remember may be uplifting, beautiful and interesting, but these four are the practice of purification.

It takes right view to realize that this is what one needs to do and that a lot of work is necessary in that direction. There are very few people in the world who never have unwholesome thoughts. Because of these unwholesome thoughts we have an unwholesome world to live in. It's not the buildings or the vehicles or the governments that make this world. It's the thought processes we have and are confronted with that make the difference between peace and war, inside and outside ourselves.

Labelling our thoughts means knowing what we are thinking. We have to start somewhere, and the best place to start is in meditation practice when we can notice clearly the continuous chatter in the mind. Thoughts can be wholesome or unwholesome or neutral; they can be distracted or restless, anxious or fearful, hateful or envious, or totally foggy. Unless we make a stab at this, we are not going to get inside ourselves and we'll never find out why we feel and act the way we do.

The four supreme efforts are the essence of the spiritual path. Flowers and incense, candles and bells, temples and dagobas are only pleasant embellishments. 'Not to let an unwholesome thought arise which has not yet arisen. Not to let it continue when it has arisen. To make a wholesome thought arise which has not yet arisen. To make a wholesome thought continue which has already arisen.' That's the purification process in thought which brings about purification in speech and action. When that happens one sees more clearly. A pure mirror with a clean surface, free from dust and dirt, is one that reflects a pure image.

Effort is needed for whatever we do, especially for meditation. The effort in meditation often doesn't seem to bring any immediate results. Because of that the mind is unable to resurrect the effort because it wants to see some results. This is attachment, clinging and wanting. It's desire and therefore suffering.

This applies to whatever we do. We have expectations of results and when they are not fulfilled, dejection and depression arise. Effort is made for effort's sake and not for results' sake. To make right effort is wholesome and beneficial in itself. If effort is made in the right direction, it is good kamma without having to show specific and expected results. If there is no immediately visible and noticeable result from meditation, good kamma is made in any case because of the wholesome intention.

Right effort brings its own reward, but we hardly ever notice this. We're expecting something tangible. 'I've been trying so hard and I still can't get concentrated,' or, 'I've been so loving to my children and they don't appreciate it,' or 'I've looked after my ailing aunt for so long and she never has a nice word to say about it.' This is the wrong way of looking at it. The effort made *is* the good kamma, *is* the result. What other people say or what other results there may be, is a secondary consideration. Sometimes one really achieves concentration. Sometimes somebody really appreciates what one has done. But that has no bearing on the efficacy of one's effort. If we don't see it that way, our effort will always be dependent upon results. It will come and go because results come and go. If effort does not remain constant, it's obviously going to be much less effective. Right effort has to be steady.

Right Mindfulness

The next step is right mindfulness. Any time you may have practised it, you may have become aware of what it means. If one puts one's foot down on the ground and knows nothing else except that the foot has been put down on the ground, that is mindfulness. When one puts the spoon in one's mouth and knows nothing else except putting the spoon in one's mouth, that is mindfulness. This feels quite different from the ordinary way of everyday living, and unless you have known that difference, you haven't yet practised mindfulness. At the moment of complete mindfulness, there is also complete oblivion to everything else. It's one-pointed. That one-pointedness takes care of letting go of problems because one can't think of two things at once. That one-pointedness, when used in meditation, eventually creates blissful absorption. In daily living it takes care of problems which are no longer uppermost in the mind, and in meditation it creates bliss. What more can it do?

It can also help to purify. When one actually knows what one is doing, saying and thinking, one is going to be very careful that it is all wholesome and that one is not over-whelmed by an impetuous, unwholesome reaction. In this way purification takes place.

Sometimes there is confusion about what 'right' mindfulness means. I've heard it said that right mindfulness is directed only towards that which is right and proper. That's not logical. Right mindfulness means that one is aware and attentive all the time. How would one ever change that which is not whole-some, if one has not paid attention to it and is oblivious to its existence?

The four foundations of mindfulness are: mindfulness of the body – its actions, its movements, its breath, its thirty-two parts, its skeleton, its corpse; mindfulness of feeling – the physical sensations or the emotional feelings; mindfulness of thought – thinking processes, knowing that the thinking is going on, knowing that the mind is working, knowing that there is a thought, knowing the thought; and the fourth one, mindfulness of mind objects – knowing whether the thought is wholesome or unwholesome.

Traditionally, mindfulness of mind objects is explained as knowing whether any of the five hindrances, the seven factors of enlightenment, any of the path-factors of the noble eightfold path or any of the six sense contacts have arisen. But in practical terms and for everyday usage, that's a bit cumbersome. Most people don't remember all the points against which to check. It's sufficient to know whether the thought has been wholesome or unwholesome. Obviously all four foundations can't be practised at once. In meditation we pick and choose. We either watch the in- and out-breath or do walking meditation, which both belong to mindfulness of the body. Or we may use mindfulness of feeling and sensa-tions. If we realize that we have been disturbed by thinking, that's mindfulness of the thought process. When we give the thought a name and realize it's either hate or dislike or love and compassion, we are using mindfulness of the mind ob-jects. So we choose in meditation where we want to put our attention.

In daily living it's not quite like that. There we have to put our attention on what's momentarily appropriate. If we cross a busy street and keep our attention strictly on our steps, it's not going to be a skilful means of staying alive. We will have to watch what the cars are doing. In this case we have to become aware of what's going on around us. If we're talking on the telephone, it's not likely that we should put our atten-tion on how we are holding the receiver. If we did that, we wouldn't know what to say. We have to keep our attention on the thinking process and the speech which results from that. Whatever is appropriate, that's where the attention is.

Mindfulness is the one mental factor which can and must be practised in every waking moment. There are twenty-four hours in the day and we might, if all goes well, meditate one hour in the morning and one hour at night. We might sleep six or seven hours, which leaves us with at least fifteen hours in the day. If we forget about being mindful for those fifteen hours in the day, we might as well forget about meditating and about practising the Buddha's teaching. We are only paying lip service.

When mindfulness is established as a practice, it eventually becomes a habit, which makes life smooth because one is able to avoid pitfalls. It works like a brake on a motorcar. It's dangerous to drive a car without brakes. If we live life without mindfulness it's equally risky. We're constantly in danger of colliding with someone and hurting ourselves and others.

When mindfulness is practised it doesn't mean that we are submissive and react in the way others expect. That's not mindfulness, that's compliance. Mindfulness is knowing what we're feeling, thinking and doing. When we know that, we become aware of our reactions. We are not concerned with acting in accordance with expectations. We are concerned with the purification of ourselves.

Right effort – the four supreme efforts – can only be successful if coupled with mindfulness. All the path factors need mindfulness as a support.

Mindfulness goes together with clear comprehension. Mindfulness is the knowing factor – simply knowing – expressed succinctly in a Japanese haiku which goes like this:

The old pond.
The frog jumps in.
Plop.

When a frog jumps into a pond, many things happen, the water ripples, the frog disappears, there might be sunshine glistening on the drops of water. All these are extraneous. Mindfulness goes to the essence, to the point, and that's 'plop.' That's all that really happened. That's the essence.

That's knowing only, which has as its companion clear comprehension. Clear comprehension understands what has happened and how to make use of it. Clear comprehension can be said to consist of three parts: knowing the purpose; knowing whether one is using skilful means; and knowing whether one has actually achieved one's purpose.

Whenever we speak without purpose, mindfulness and clear comprehension have been abandoned. When we speak with a purpose but don't know how to express ourselves, we have no skilful means at our disposal. If we don't get the results we want, we obviously haven't used the right means. Mindfulness in speech and action needs clear comprehension as its companion: knowing the purpose, the skilful means and the results. When we live with mindfulness there is a marked difference in our awareness. We know what's happening with ourselves but we don't become involved in it. When anger arises we know it's arising, but we don't have to become angry. That's a great skill. When there is boredom, we know boredom has arisen, but we don't have to become bored or frustrated. We just know the arising and also the ceasing of all mental states.

Mindfulness is available to everyone and is used by everyone for survival, but since survival is a lost cause, we might as well use some more mindfulness in order to become liberated and free. Mindfulness *is* the skilful means and clear comprehension, the wisdom that can discriminate. Mindfulness is non-judgemental, but clear comprehension has the aspect of differentiating, so we can change our direction if necessary.

Right Concentration

Right concentration is found in the meditative absorptions which are mentioned by the Buddha in discourse after discourse as the way and the means, but not as the goal. They provide a pleasant abiding, he says, a pleasant way of living and working for insight. If one gets attached to them one just has another attachment, added to the many one has already. However, the meditative absorptions are the necessary means for getting the mind into shape to see clearly.

Right concentration needs all the other factors of the noble eightfold path as a base. Without moral conduct, right intention and right view, right effort and right mindfulness, it cannot arise. Because it needs all of those, it's mentioned at the end. Also because it is the one that can get us to the point of departure, from being a worldling to becoming a noble person. Right view stands at the beginning because without it nothing happens. Right concentration stands at the end because it needs all the other factors in order to function and constitutes the means for achieving penetrating insight.

When right concentration has succeeded and a deliberate attempt at insight has been made, right view arises. This will be the right view of liberation. At the end we have come full circle to right view of self, which means non-self. We cannot find non-self. We cannot find what isn't there. Therefore we can only constantly inquire into what we believe to be self. We believe body, feelings, perception, mental formations and our sense consciousness to be self. We need to inquire into anything that appears to be 'me.' Unless we have 'self' fully in hand, are master of it and have seen it fully, we will not be able to let go of it. If I don't know where my clock is, if I don't have it in hand, I can't give it away. Only if I know exactly what and where it is, can I let go of it. If I'm looking for the clock and can't find it, there is nothing I can do about it. The same applies to 'self.'

The inquiry is into 'me.' What is this body? Is it really 'me' and 'mine'? If it becomes a corpse, is it still mine? Am I going to say this is 'my' corpse? Who's going to say, 'This is my corpse'? This is the line of inquiry. Are these feelings really mine? Why do I get the ones I don't want? Who's making them come? Why do I get a pain in my right knee? Why do I get all the thoughts I don't want? Why do I get thoughts that make me unhappy? *Who* is getting unhappy? Who is this 'me'? Was 'me' yesterday or was 'me' today or is 'me' tomorrow? Any line of inquiry to find out *where* is 'me,' *what* is 'me.' And when I finally find it, then I can let go of the delusion.

The inquiry into 'non-self' has to start with the inquiry into 'self' and as it becomes more and more obvious that there's some misconception about 'self,' it also becomes clearer that the thinking process can use different channels.

All the factors we have spoken about are ways and means

of diminishing ego, making it a bit smaller. Concentration is an important aspect, because at the time when the mind is fully concentrated, there's no thought of 'I am, I can, I will be, I want, I don't want.' When the meditative absorptions are practised regularly the 'I' is often diminished and one can see a little more clearly. As long as we have practised neither concentration nor mindfulness, the ego takes itself for granted and remains its usual normal size, as big as people around one will allow. With mindfulness and concentration, that changes.

The noble eightfold path goes from relative right view to absolute right view and in the end, one becomes the noble eightfold path. There is no need to practise it any more at that point nor to try to remember it. No need to make effort with each step, because the noble eightfold path has become one's natural way of being. The Arahant has constant right view and right intention. There can be no wrong speech, wrong action or wrong livelihood. There is always right effort, right mindfulness and right concentration. With us, a little bit at a time. Only practice makes perfect.

13   *A New Beginning*

You've been here for ten days and are going home to an entirely different situation. Your meditation has markedly improved and also your understanding of the Buddha's teaching. When you get home, you might think that the people at home have changed. All of a sudden they don't seem to understand what you are saying. They're concerned with things that don't seem very important. You can be sure it's not they who have changed, it's you.

When you get to town and watch people and traffic, the thought might occur to you, 'What's everybody rushing for? Where are they all going? What's the hurry?' You stand still, look and think, 'I can't understand what the hurry is all about?' In about three weeks or three months, depending on your practice, it may all look completely normal to you again. That's what everybody does, and that means that you're doing it too. That will be a sure indication that your practice has lapsed, your introspection has gone and you need to go to another retreat.

So what to do about all this? Meditate one hour in the morning and one hour at night, which is a general recipe. If you can spend more time in meditation, so much the better.

In practical terms you can do several things. You have a place in your house where you sleep, eat, cook and bathe. Designate a place for meditation and don't change it. You don't change your dining area and you don't move your bedroom. Likewise keep a meditation corner big enough to accommodate you and a pillow. Put a pillow or a mat there to sit on and leave it there. If you have to search for it, there is already distraction. You might like to have a Buddha statue or some flowers or a picture in your corner to give it the appropriate aspect. Just as a dining room has table and chairs, and your kitchen has a stove, so your meditation corner has a pillow and possibly a shrine, or just flowers or a candle.

Go to your corner to meditate every day at exactly the same time and take a clock with you, one that doesn't tick and has an alarm. Set the alarm for one hour because if you don't, you're going to sit there meditating and you'll think, 'Well, that's at least an hour now.' When you get up and go to the kitchen, you find it's only ten minutes, and once you're up and in the kitchen, you're not going to go back. Nobody does that. So have an alarm and even when you think, 'That must be an hour,' you know it can't be, because the alarm hasn't rung yet. Just as you know here when the little bell hasn't rung yet, that the time isn't up. Even though you'd like to get up, everybody else is sitting, so you sit too. Eventually the meditation comes together.

We need all the help we can get. We're always looking for the easy way out. Everybody is. Be aware of the easy way out. Nobody would have sat here as often and as long as we did if we hadn't all sat here together. It's very helpful to have a group of meditators even if only two friends come together. Two make a group. If they don't know how to meditate, tell them about loving-kindness meditation and watching the breath, and then sit together.

However, don't try to convince anybody in your family that they must practise too. That's the sure way of turning them off. Just say, 'I like it. I'm going to do it.' That's enough. Who can argue about that? And 'I'm going to get up an hour earlier.' Great. You get up nicely, quietly, not waking anybody up because you don't want them running around talking and you sit in the corner and you do your meditation. What could be simpler than that? In the evening, come to your corner whatever time you can. Wait until the television has been turned off for the evening.

We are habit-prone in our mind. When we were small, our mothers used to tell us, 'Go and clean your teeth.' And we used to say, 'I don't want to,' or 'I did already,' or 'Why should I?' or 'I'll do it later.' But she kept insisting, 'Go and clean your teeth.' Eventually we did go and year after year she kept insisting, until today we're still cleaning our teeth. Here you have to be your own mother. When the mind says,

'I don't want to,' or 'I'll do that meditation later,' or 'What could one day matter?' or 'I'll do it tomorrow,' or 'It's too strenuous. My knees hurt,' don't listen, say, 'Go! Go and sit. It's the only thing that's really worthwhile doing.' When we were small, we didn't know why we had to clean our teeth. Mother kept saying they're all going to fall out, but we didn't know what that meant. How can teeth fall out, we thought. But now we're being told, 'If you don't meditate, you're not going to have a mind that can actually function properly.' Well, maybe we don't really know how a mind cannot function properly. Just tell yourself like a mother, 'This is good for you. Go on, do it.' You have to look after your mind. If you don't, it will not look after you.

This habit is beneficial and wholesome, and constitutes the path of purity. Our habitual thinking forms our character and directs us into spiritual endeavours and pathways.

If we don't use each day for anything other than trying to stay alive and entertaining ourselves, it's a waste of time. Certainly we have to stay alive, otherwise we can't meditate, but that need not take our full attention and priority. We have to add the ingredient of mindfulness and practise it all the waking hours of the day. Whatever we do – cooking, cleaning, shopping or walking – can be a lesson in mindfulness. When washing dishes don't think what to do next when this boring task is done, but keep the mind totally together with the physical action. When cleaning floors don't think how to get out of doing it, but be attentive to each movement; that's mindfulness.

All negative thoughts are degenerating for the mind. Just as the body degenerates from wear and tear, so does the mind. It becomes a less wholesome mind with every unskilful thought. Whenever there is 'I don't like it. I don't want it. I want to get out of it. I hate it. I'm jealous. I'm proud of it' in the mind, we become a weaker person, having lost our mindfulness and clear comprehension once more.

Mindfulness can be directed to our physical actions, to our feelings, to our thoughts or to the contents of the thoughts, whichever one of the four is appropriate at the moment. When there's a feeling of sadness, for example, attention is directed to that feeling with the realization that it will not bring any kind of benefit to anyone. We learn to either substitute or drop it. When there is thinking going on, being fully aware that there is a thought process, and then knowing the content. This means knowing whether it's wholesome or unwholesome.

This too becomes habit, and prevents us from blaming others. It cleans the cobwebs out of the thinking processes and makes them clear. We know what is going on inside ourselves and around us, internally and externally.

It's at least a fifteen-hour-a-day job, depending on how long one sleeps at night. Unless this job is done during all or most of one's waking hours, one cannot hope to meditate successfully. Unless one meditates, one cannot hope to achieve mindfulness. The two are totally interdependent. Meditation has to be pursued whether one considers it successful or not. It's a matter of patience, endurance, determination and perseverance. One just has to sit and do it.

During your ten days here you had an excellent opportunity to sit and do it and that has brought results. At home, where there's much less time for meditation the results may not be the same, nor may they improve. Concentration is a fragile achievement. It needs to be nurtured and cared for the way it deserves. Real concentration is a jewel that very few people in this world get to know. They may read or hear about it but that doesn't give them the benefit of it. It's meaningless unless one experiences it and this rare achievement needs to be treated with the reverence it deserves; namely constant application to keep it going.

Concentrated meditation will also facilitate mindfulness during the day. For anyone who hasn't attained the advanced stage known as stream-entry, about half of what arises in the mind is unwholesome. When one becomes aware of this, then one can drop it because one has learned to do that in meditation.

We need to be wary of fuzzy, unaware living. The miracle of being awake is not the opposite of being asleep. It's the opposite of being unaware. Many of us have no understanding of what we're doing, thinking or feeling. We are taking the easy way out, being half asleep. This is an escape from suffering. Knowing suffering means knowing the truth, the first noble truth of Lord Buddha. Anyone who wants to get rid of suffering must first inquire into it. Knowing suffering and not trying to escape would be foolish. There is no escape route externally or through non-attention or non-awareness. The only escape is through insight, which brings total clarity. Every other escape route is blocked.

Once a week meditate together with some friends. It boosts the individual effort. Group energy has a certain momentum. What makes life difficult for us are our defilements, the five hindrances. The one antidote that is the same for all five is noble friends and noble conversation. Don't fall in with *any* conversation. You wouldn't eat anything that might be poisonous, likewise don't take anything into your mind that might be harmful, such as gossip, idle chatter or slander, what the media usually hand out, cheap novels, talking for talking's sake. It will poison the mind and take you in the wrong direction.

Another way of being imbued with Dhamma is seeing every situation, every experience – be it ever so small and insignificant – in the way of Dhamma. When you see a bush with beautiful flowers and there are also a number of dead flowers on the same bush, the mind should revert to birth, decay, disease and death. Or you may see birds building a nest, and being very careful, taking so many pains to make it snug and comfortable. In the next tree there may be an abandoned nest. Constant flux and flow. Nothing permanent. There's my nest, my house. So much money, energy, time is expended on this nest. One day it will be empty and abandoned by me.

Everything around you externally can be seen in the way of Dhamma, having no solidity, no stability, no core essence, and therefore always being unsatisfactory. That does not create morbidity or sadness. On the contrary it alleviates grief and pain by taking the heaviness out of all that happens. It creates a lessening of desire because one sees that the gratification of the desire will not bring fulfilment, since all this is changing anyway.

The real Dhamma lives in the heart. It can't live in temples, robes or Bodhi trees. There is only one place Dhamma can live. Those who have taken the Dhamma to heart and are practising, they are the temples of the Dhamma. The temples are made from brick and plaster. The Bodhi tree cannot live as an example, it's a symbol and so is a statue. We need symbols, because we're constantly forgetting. They are reminders. But the real Dhamma has to be in the heart where it can come to life.

The Buddha said, 'Whoever sees me, sees Dhamma. Whoever sees Dhamma, sees me.' At this time in the history of humanity, we have no chance of seeing a live Buddha, but it's not necessary because 'Whoever sees Dhamma, sees me.' If you can see the Dhamma in your own heart, you can see the Buddha. Buddha means nothing but enlightenment. It means the Awakened One. Once you see Dhamma in your own heart, that is what you will see and that is what you want, isn't it? Seeing the live Buddha. He is as near to you as your own heart. He couldn't be any nearer. You don't have to go anywhere to find him. You don't have to do anything special to find it. You just have to be mindful and change the unwholesome to the wholesome. Isn't that simple? But because it is so simple it doesn't mean that it is easy. It's hard work but it's the kind of work that brings the greatest profit. There is nothing to compare with it. You have all the necessary tools. They are all yours. Now you must use them.

Glossary

The following Pāli words encompass concepts and levels of ideas for which there are no adequate synonyms in English. The explanations of these terms have been adapted from the *Buddhist Dictionary* by Nyanatiloka Mahathera.

Anatta 'No-self,' non-ego, egolessness, impersonality; 'neither within the bodily and mental phenomena of existence, nor outside of them can be found anything that in the ultimate sense could be regarded as a self-existing real ego-identity, soul or any other abiding substance.'

Anicca 'Impermanent,' a basic feature of all conditioned phenomena, be they material or mental, coarse or subtle, one's own or external.

Arahant 'The Liberated One'; one who has realized the forth and final fruit of liberation, by which he has destroyed all mental defilements and attained release from the round of rebirth.

Dhamma The liberating law discovered and proclaimed by the Buddha, summed up in the Four Noble Truths.

Dukkha (1) In common usage: 'Pain,' painful feeling, which may be bodily or mental; (2) In Buddhist usage as, e.g. in the Four Noble Truths: 'suffering,' 'ill,' the unsatisfactory nature and the general insecurity of all conditioned phenomena. Hence 'unsatisfactoriness' or 'liability to suffering' would be more adequate renderings.

Jhāna Meditative absorptions. Tranquillity meditation.

Kamma 'Action,' denotes the wholesome and unwholesome volitions and their concomitant mental factors, causing rebirth and shaping the character of beings and thereby their destiny. The term by no means signifies the result of actions, and quite certainly not the deterministic fate of humanity.

Khandha   The Five 'Groups' are the five aspects in which the Buddha has summed up all the physical and mental phenomena of existence, and which appear to the ordinary person as his ego, or personality, to wit 1) Body (*rupa*), 2) Feeling (*vedana*), 3) Perception (*sañña*), 4) Mental Formations (*sankhāra*), 5) Consciousness (*viññana*).

Mettā   All embracing loving-kindness.

Nibbāna   Nibbāna constitutes the highest and ultimate goal of all Buddhist aspirations, i.e. absolute extinction of that life-affirming will manifested as Greed, Hate and Delusion, and convulsively clinging to existence; and therewith also the ultimate and absolute deliverance from all future rebirth, old age, disease and death, from all suffering and misery.

Samsāra   'Round of Rebirth,' lit. 'perpetual wandering,' is a name by which is designated the sea of life ever restlessly heaving up and down; the symbol of this continuous process of ever, again and again, being born, growing old, suffering and dying.

Sangha   In the ordinary sense, the community of monks and nuns; in a higher sense, the community of noble ones. In this second sense, the Sangha is the third of the Three Jewels and the Three Refuges.

Vipassanā   Insight into the truth of the impermanence, suffering and impersonality of all corporeal and mental phenomena of existence.

Other Wisdom Books from the Theravadin Tradition

Ven. Dr. H. Saddhatissa
BUDDHIST ETHICS
The Path to Nirvana

A Theravadin scholar and monk of over fifty years lucidly examines Buddhist doctrines, the Three Jewels, Buddhist Scriptures, the position of the laity in Buddhism and the importance of taking responsibility for our actions towards others. This thorough assessment clearly reveals the relationship between Buddhist ethics and the ultimate goal of Nirvana.

216pp, £6.95/$12.95

A Wisdom Basic Book · Orange Series

Other Wisdom Books from the Theravadin
Tradition

THUS HAVE I HEARD
The Long Discourses of the Buddha
Translated by Maurice Walshe

Thus Have I Heard is a new translation of the *Digha
Nikaya,* a collection of the thirty-four long discourses
(suttas) given by the Buddha in India two and a half
thousand years ago. These suttas — some of the
most popular scriptures in the Pali Canon — reveal
the gentleness, compassion, power and penetrating
wisdom of the Buddha.

    Venerable Sumedho Thera writes in his foreword:
'They are not meant to be "sacred scriptures" that
tell us what to believe. One should read them, listen
to them, think about them, contemplate them and
investigate the present reality, the present experience
with them. Then, and only then, can one insightfully
know the truth beyond words.'

648pp, £17.95/$34.95

A Wisdom Intermediate Book · White Series

Other Wisdom Books from the Tibetan
Buddhist Tradition

Geshe Namgyal Wangchen
AWAKENING THE MIND OF
ENLIGHTENMENT
Meditations on the Buddhist Path

As society becomes increasingly materialistic, the
need for a balancing degree of inner awareness and
compassionate motivation in our lives becomes more
and more obvious. The Buddhist meditation
tradition offers profound and effective methods for
developing these qualities in a gradual way with the
ultimate goal of awakening the mind of
enlightenment.

This book is a simple, clear presentation of
meditations that take the beginner to that goal.
Written in English by a contemporary Tibetan
Buddhist master, it skilfully presents the traditional
teachings of the *lam-rim* (graduated path) for Western
people, and is an ideal guide not just for beginners,
but also for those who wish to refresh their minds
with the stages of practice.

264pp, £7.95/$14.95

A Wisdom Basic Book · Orange Series

Other Wisdom Books from the Tibetan
Buddhist Tradition

THE JEWEL IN THE LOTUS
A Guide to the Buddhist Traditions of Tibet
Edited by Stephen Batchelor

This is the first book in English to bring together a
clear and down-to-earth introduction to Tibetan
Buddhism along with selections of teachings from
each of its major traditions.

Stephen Batchelor's introduction provides the
historical background to Tibetan Buddhism and
explains the main doctrines common to all four
schools — the Nyingma, Kagyu, Sakya and Gelug
— as well as the earlier Kadam. The extracts, which
include teachings from the present Dalai Lama,
Atisha, Longchen Rabjampa, Ngorchen Kunga
Zangpo, Je Tzong Khapa and Jetsun Milarepa,
illustrate on the one hand the diversity and different
emphasis of each school, and on the other the
undeniable unity of all traditions — as a slightly
different route to the same goal, enlightenment.

280pp, £9.95/$18.95

A Wisdom Basic Book · Orange Series

Other Wisdom Books from our East-West
Series

Joel Levey
THE FINE ARTS OF RELAXATION,
CONCENTRATION AND MEDITATION
Ancient Skills for Modern Minds

For fifteen years, Joel Levey, a Buddhist and stress
management consultant, has worked with thousands
of people in the areas of business, education, health
care, sports and the military.

Included here are more than a hundred of the
techniques that he has found most beneficial in his
work. They combine the strengths of modern day
medical technology and the ancient skills of
relaxation, concentration and meditation, making
this book a very practical mental fitness manual.

232pp, £7.95/$14.95

A Wisdom East-West Book · Grey Series

Other Wisdom Books from our East-West
Series

Radmila Moacanin
JUNG'S PSYCHOLOGY AND TIBETAN
BUDDHISM
Western and Eastern Paths to the Heart

In *Jung's Psychology and Tibetan Buddhism* Radmila
Moacanin reconciles an ancient Eastern spiritual
discipline with a contemporary Western
psychological system. She touches on many of their
major ideas and methods and finds that, although
there are fundamental differences, both are vitally
concerned with what Jung called "the tremendous
experiment of becoming conscious," successfully
bridging the gap between our deepest yearnings for
spiritual fulfilment and the demands of our mundane
life.

128pp, £6.95/$12.95

A Wisdom East-West Book · Grey Series